Set Good Boundaries

Where You Stop, and I Begin

Zera Young

Get Your Ebook Stop Limiting Yourself
+ Reduce Stress in 1 minute [video]
+ Printable Gratitude Journal

Scan the QR code below to claim your free bonuses

———————————— OR ————————————

visit gifts.zerayoung.com/boundaries

Scan me

Get Ready to Live a Life With No Limits!

- ✓ Free e-book: Stop Limiting Yourself. Stop doubting your potential and learn to recognize your self-limiting beliefs!
- ✓ Free meditation video: Reduce your stress levels in one minute with this powerful breathing exercise.
- ✓ Printable Journal: Print out your daily and monthly Personal Gratitude Journal for positive manifestation and improved self-confidence!

Get My Audiobook for FREE

If you love listening to audiobooks on the go, you can download the audiobook version of my book *Set Good Boundaries* for FREE (Regularly $14.95) just by signing up for a FREE 30-day Audible trial!

Follow the QR codes below to get started

Audible US

Audible UK

Contents

Introduction

"Connection is why we're here. We are hardwired to connect with others, it's what gives purpose and meaning to our lives, and without it there is suffering."

— Brené Brown

– We all have a deep need for belonging and feeling connected to others. Human nature predisposes us to form bonds of attachment. It's a survival instinct and one of the most powerful dynamics between humans that has allowed us to multiply and thrive. Parents have a primal understanding that they must care for their child if it is to survive. A child naturally forms an attachment to the caregiver who ensures its survival needs are met. This is the first deep human connection we establish and, as we grow, this primal need for attachment evolves. As Brené Brown describes beautifully in the quote above, we are hardwired for attachment and a sense of belonging.

But attachment is not the only fundamental need we have as humans. As children, and later as adults, we have an equally important desire for authenticity. Authenticity is about recognizing your own strengths, accepting who you are, and having the courage and self-confidence to share this with the world. This is where boundaries come in. Boundaries define us. They protect our time, energy, health, and peace. They aren't about keeping things out, but about protecting what's inside.

When these two fundamental needs (attachment and authenticity) are completely in balance, we can be genuinely supportive of others without sacrificing our own needs. In many cases, however, we choose attachment (or approval and recognition from others) over authenticity. We, understandably, deem it more important for others to like us than to speak our truth. Frankly, it can be easier to sweep our thoughts, feelings, and desires under the rug in an effort to please the people around us.

We are in a constant dilemma to be authentic while at the same time trying to nurture our attachment to others. This interplay between authenticity and our primal need for attachment is where tension arises and our vision gets blurred when it comes to setting healthy boundaries.

Boundaries aren't like physical borders around countries—we can't see them, touch them, or run into them, so how do we make sure they're there? Knowing ourselves and communicating with others is a great start. We have to be aware of our metaphorical on-and-off switch: What makes us feel good in a relationship and what makes us feel bad?

The problem often lies in the fact that people feel more comfortable bending their own boundaries to satisfy someone else's needs, rather than simply telling them 'no'. It is only through understanding the importance of boundaries that we will be able to actually take that step. Otherwise, we will continue living in our comfort zones, allowing others to take advantage of our kindness, time, and energy. If we don't set boundaries for ourselves, someone else will set them for us. We will agree to things we don't want to do, give up our autonomy, and forfeit our own satisfaction. And in the worst case, we lose touch with our true selves.

It's easy to blame others for taking more than they give, but we must learn to take control of our own destiny. Setting boundaries is key to safeguarding your authentic self, but if we are to master the craft of saying "no" more often, we must first examine the reasons why we limit ourselves in this way.

Establishing boundaries in your relationships isn't a change that can be made overnight. It takes time to build up your confidence, courage, and willpower to establish and clearly express your limits. Our unique experiences, preferences, and morals influence the way we want our relationships to be. These aspects require some deep self-reflection in order for us to become aware of our boundaries and adjust our relationships accordingly.

By declaring that our happiness is in our own hands, we transfer that responsibility onto ourselves. It might seem scary to realize the success of your life depends on you, but it is the better alternative. It allows you to take the steps—no matter how difficult—to stop letting others drain you.

Boundaries will open up a whole new chapter of your life that you might have been deprived of this whole time. They will make space for you to live the life you want and cultivate relationships that allow you to grow into the best version of yourself.

By the end of this book, you will have all the tools you need to start enjoying the countless benefits of having carved out space for YOU to thrive. To list a few:

- Increased independence and gaining happiness and fulfillment from within
- Improved self-esteem
- Ability to focus on your own well-being
- Allow your authentic needs space to thrive
- Prevent being taken advantage of by others
- Become more assertive and say 'no' when needed
- Prevent social/relationship burnout

The list goes on and on. Boundaries are essential. Your life is likely shaped by boundaries you may not even be aware of. This book is about much more than simply teaching you to say 'no' - it is meant to help you understand the complex dynamics at play in all your relationships and free you from the burden of pleasing others.

Chapter 1
What are Boundaries?

Each time you set a healthy boundary, you say 'yes' to more freedom.

— Nancy Levin

- Some people define boundaries as our basic moral compass. This means they would include rules such as no cheating, no lying, respecting others' time by not being late to events, or being honest about your feelings. To others, boundaries cover aspects that are less about moral standards and more about personal preferences. The foundation of any healthy relationship consists of comfort, safety, and trust. These three aspects look different depending on whom you ask, so to understand how to establish boundaries, you must first evaluate what things have to be in place in order for you to feel secure and happy in your relationships.

Many people will base their boundaries around some of their previous experiences. If they were often yelled at as a child, then being yelled at by other people (even as an adult) can trigger some harmful memories and bring up feelings of being unsafe. Yelling is usually a red flag in any relationship —it demonstrates a lack of respect, an inability to control emotions, and a failure to participate in mature conversations. However, to some people, yelling is considerably more traumatizing and much more of a deal breaker than it is to others. Some people wouldn't cut a friend off just because they raised their voice a few times, but other people certainly would.

Another example could be a friendship or relationship where one wants to spend a lot of time together while the other person feels smothered. Some people simply *love* to surround themselves with people all the time while others place a greater value on their alone time or doing things independently.

This goes to show that boundaries aren't solely representative of the morals you hold. It doesn't have to be only about what you believe is right and wrong—it can also be simply about how you want to be treated.

Types of Boundaries

Let's get into the thick of it and explore the different forms of boundaries. There are seven different types (Martin, 2020):

1. **Physical boundaries.** Physical boundaries are meant to provide you with a safe space. They range anywhere from being entitled to basic

resources such as food and water, to specific things that make you feel secure. Asking people to not open your closet is a physical boundary, as is asking people to not sit too close to you. Physical boundaries convey that you are the *only one* who gets to decide how your body and personal space can be treated.

2. **Sexual boundaries.** These boundaries can be of sexual or romantic nature. Due to its naturally touchy subject, many people are very well aware of what sexual boundaries they have but are scared to communicate and maintain them. Sexual boundaries should cover everything you *are* and *aren't* comfortable with; in other words, how far you are willing to go sexually. For example: how often you are willing to have sex, what positions you are and aren't willing to try out, and how and where you would like to be touched or not. Sexual boundaries should be very firm and completely understood by your partner(s); make sure to prevent any possible grey areas and get very clear on your preferences and limits with each other. Don't forget that sexual boundaries can be dynamic. You might suddenly feel uncomfortable and change your mind, and that's perfectly fine.

3. **Emotional and mental boundaries.** With emotional and mental boundaries (lumped together into one single category), you are effectively taking power over your thoughts and feelings; seems like this is a given fact, right? Well, these boundaries go beyond just stating the obvious. They form the barrier between your own emotions and the emotions experienced by others.

In other words, while you are responsible for how you are feeling, you are not responsible for how others feel. This applies to many situations, including those in which the behavior of someone else makes you feel unpleasant. For example, if your sibling likes to one-up you every time you express your feelings, you could kindly explain to them that their experience does not invalidate yours. Another instance could be if someone always dumps their trauma on you as a form of 'friendship bonding'—you could let them know that while you understand their experience, you cannot be emotionally responsible to console them at all times. Their pain is not your burden to bear.

4. **Spiritual and religious boundaries.**
Spiritual and religious boundaries go both ways: for the person that has faith in a set of beliefs as well as for the person that does not hold that same faith. If you are a religious or spiritual person, the people you hold relationships with should respect that and allow you to believe and practice your faith even if they do not. On the flip side, if you are not a religious or spiritual person and someone in your life cannot accept that, they will likely try over and over again to push their personal beliefs onto you. In this case, you are also entitled to set a religious boundary by making it clear that you want them to stop trying to change your belief system.

5. **Financial and material boundaries.**
Money is the root of all evil, right? Well, I would disagree. I say that what money does to people is the root of all evil and not the money itself. In a lot

of cases, money is indeed the root of many problems in family relationships, romantic relationships, and even friendships. Financial boundaries allow you to be in full control of your finances: where you want to spend your money, how you want to earn it, whom you want to lend it to, and how much you want to save. With this boundary, you are not allowing others to treat your money as their own. The same concept is applied to material boundaries—you are the only one who ultimately decides how a material object of yours gets to be treated. Examples could look like saying "No, I cannot lend you another $1,000," or "Please, ask me first before you borrow my laptop."

6. **Time boundaries.** In my belief, time is the most valuable resource of all since we can't get it back, no matter how hard we try. For this reason, we should be putting extra care into making sure that our time stays ours. To nourish and maintain equal relationships you must keep full ownership of your time. Setting a time boundary will prevent those around you from exploiting it. You could tell your friend that you cannot hang out with them all weekend because you have other things to do. The same can be applied if someone always asks you to help them with tasks over and over again—your time is yours and it is okay to say no, even if you don't have a clear reason.

7. **Non-negotiable boundaries.** Non-negotiable boundaries are a category of their own, but they are often one of the previously mentioned six types. The name might speak for itself, but non-negotiable boundaries are those that signify a

dealbreaker for a relationship. Non-negotiable boundaries make us feel safe. If you are a monogamous person and your partner cheats on you, they have likely broken a non-negotiable boundary. If your friend refuses to be careful while driving, you will probably stop getting into a car with them. The people in your life should be aware of the concrete non-negotiable boundaries you have. We must be careful not to place too many of our boundaries in this category. You must be prepared to stick to your non-negotiables for them to have any significance.

As you start to get a sense of these various types of boundaries, you can begin to examine your own. In a lot of cases, people prevent themselves from exploring what is possible when it comes to boundaries. Many of us have been taught from a young age that certain boundaries are invalid or selfish. We will explore this further in the next few chapters, but there is nothing narcissistic and self-serving about setting boundaries with those around you.

Knowing What to Look For

Many people who did not grow up being meticulously taught about boundaries (so, most of us) are likely to interpret them as something cold when in reality, "maintaining boundaries is about being the gatekeeper of your life in order to keep yourself safe and well," (Nitka, 2020). What many people don't realize is that they already have boundaries that are unique to them. They are simply unaware of what exactly those boundaries are, and as such find themselves unable to communicate them effectively to others.

Mina was a client of mine. She had a longtime friend, Richard, with a short fuse. From the sounds of it, you wouldn't want to be near Richard when his anger took over, and he had become prone to directing his rage toward Mina during heartfelt conversations. Mina ruminated as to how her friend could suddenly become so cruel toward her. This crossed a line, but she wasn't sure how to address it after so many years of friendship. They had always mended the relationship after such episodes and she had never felt threatened by him, but Mina had reached the end of her rope and was considering cutting all ties. Experience tells me there is likely some trauma lurking underneath explosive outbursts of rage, so we dug deeper.

Understanding the root of her friend's behavior was the first step toward Mina feeling empowered to assert herself. Exploring what provoked Richard, it became clear that his anger typically surfaced while he was airing out conflicts in his life and Mina asked questions to better understand his situation. Mina was showing she cared enough to learn more, yet he felt interrogated. Mina wanted to understand her friend but all he needed was to feel unconditionally supported. While there is a lot more to unpack here, this example points to the importance of understanding one's own boundaries.

There seemed to be a mental-emotional boundary Richard was unaware of, which led him to lash out. When he lashed out, he violated a strict boundary of Mina's, but she was hesitant to address this because she felt at fault. It wasn't necessary to determine *why* Mina's questions triggered his rage; it was enough to acknowledge that Mina could not carry on in this relationship as long as she continued to be treated this way.

Mina, armed with the awareness that this wasn't about *her* but rather about Richard's inability to control his behavior, Mina confronted the issue with her longtime friend. By communicating her own boundary, she found out that Richard had been perceiving Mina's questions as intruding on his space. He lashed out irrationally in an unnecessary defense. She placed a limit on what she would tolerate, and in doing so uncovered the trigger point of a boundary Richard had been unaware of. This didn't solve the problem overnight, but Mina had opened up the floor for an important conversation that had the power to change their relationship going forward.

Boundaries exist whether you acknowledge them or not. Maybe you don't like being hugged, maybe you feel ignored if your friend doesn't reply to a text message for several days, or perhaps you don't like discussing a certain triggering topic in conversation. We don't necessarily have to create or think up our boundaries, but rather we need to look deep within ourselves to uncover or rediscover them.

The People Who Are Good for You

We can't negate the impact people can have on our personal growth, no matter how good or bad their intentions may be. The list below serves as a good litmus test for healthy interpersonal relationships. Do a quick inventory of the people closest to you. Are your relationships with them characterized by the qualities below?

- **They are genuinely happy for you.** This one ought to be non-negotiable. If the people around you are not genuinely happy for you most of the time, they are not in this relationship for the right reasons. Do they help you celebrate your successes or does their reaction come from a place of insecurity or jealousy? Do they attribute your accomplishments to dumb luck or are they encouraging and supportive? You should not be hearing comments that negate your achievements or belittle your dreams. Constant attempts to keep you small are warning signs that someone does not have your best interest at heart.

- **They are there for you when times are rough.** It's easy to spend time with someone when both of your lives are running smoothly. What happens when things get tough? Can you rely on the support of those around you? Do you feel part of a community that has your back? When people who care about us know that we are going through a difficult time, they make themselves emotionally available for the sake of our well-being. This could come in the form of calling to check in, offering to help with an errand, or simply being there when you need to vent.

- **They are dependable and stick to their word.** Things come up, emergencies happen, and moods can change—that's understandable. You should, however, feel able to rely on the people in your life. Do they usually show up on time? Are they responsive when you reach out? What we're looking for is predictable and generally consistent behavior. Trust is a powerful bonding agent and having people around who we trust to be dependable makes us feel safe, stable, and part of a strong community.

- **They respect your differences.** Respecting another person's differences displays acceptance of their authenticity. We might not always see eye to eye with the people closest to us, but we must appreciate or try to understand their points of view. It should feel safe to disagree, and you should feel comfortable discussing your interests. Curiosity in another person's interests is a primary building block that fuels connection and deepens the bond over time.

- **They don't hold you back.** People should celebrate your success, inspire you to move forward with things that interest you, and generally support your growth. Those around you should inspire you to have faith in yourself and continuously improve your life. Someone who is stuck in a rut of their own will drain the energy and suck the motivation out of everyone around them, even without intending to do so. They may elicit your urge to enable their bad behaviors. Nobody is responsible for what life throws at them, but we all must take ownership of our path forward. Misery loves company, so don't get sucked into the vortex of another's downward spiral.

Any violation of the above is a red flag signaling the need for clearly defined boundaries in that relationship. Just as a seed needs sun and water to sprout, we must find ourselves in a supportive environment as we embark on this journey of personal growth.

Let me tell you this: surrounding yourself with the right people can change everything. Once we realize the weight of other people's influence on our lives, we can use that in our favor by pursuing new relationships that propel us toward better versions of ourselves. I have seen my life change drastically by surrounding myself with people I look up to. I began opening myself up to those who were more experienced than me or had already achieved what I wanted to achieve. Not only did their influence convince me that my dreams were realistic, but their example gave me a blueprint on how to achieve my goals.

Key Takeaways

- Boundaries are meant to create a relationship that both parties feel safe and happy in.
- Necessary boundaries will vary from person to person.
- There are seven general types of boundaries that cover different aspects of relationships.
- Our boundaries influence our relationships, whether we are aware of them or not.
- The first step in deciding which relationships in your life are worth nourishing is identifying how those people make you feel.
- People who are worth your time and energy will be happy for your success, support you when times are tough, and are dedicated to respecting you.

Chapter 2
Assessing Your Current Boundaries

The only real conflict you will ever have in your life won't be with others, but with yourself.

— Shannon L. Alder

Before we get to the meat of setting good boundaries, let's examine the boundaries already at work in your current relationships. Healthy boundaries give you space to be yourself. They protect what's inside yet allow others in only to the extent you permit. Not all boundaries are healthy, however. It is possible that some of the boundaries you already have in place could be doing more harm than good. If you feel a sense of anger or resentment, or you're simply overwhelmed in any of your relationships, there's a good chance that unhealthy boundaries are at play.

The Irony of Trust

As said by author Patrick Lencioni (2010), "teamwork begins by building trust. And the only way to do that is to overcome our need for invulnerability." A beautiful quote that captures the essence of forming boundaries: letting go of fear while ensuring your trust won't be abused.

Trust issues are a massively complex setback in relationships and can severely interfere with setting healthy boundaries. I'd argue that many of us have trust issues to one extent or another. This comes down to the fact that trust is not the safe option, and people need to feel safe.

In all transparency, trust isn't always safe. Relationships of any kind are guided by our intuition when we choose to trust, but there is likely one point or another in all our lives where our trust was misplaced. Think of people who get married to the love of their life only to be cheated on 11 years down the line or someone's childhood friend dramatically cutting ties out of the blue. Even good people make bad choices. We simply cannot predict or control other people's behavior.

On the one hand, having too much trust in others can cause you to get hurt by having boundaries that are too loose. On the other hand, having barely any trust in others means your boundaries are likely to be so rigid you never let others get close enough to truly know you. Examining your own propensity to trust and how that is interlinked with your boundaries is key to helping you better assess some areas for improvement.

An interesting 2006 study by psychologists Janine Willis and Alexander Todorov showed that people make the initial decision to trust someone within a mere 100 milliseconds of examining their face. Shocking, right? This means our brains have made up a brief template of what a trustworthy face might look like and manage to match it in real life within only a fraction of a second. We have a built-in system that can make a quick assessment of whether to trust a person or not. Based on life experience we adapt this mechanism and our risk assessment becomes more fine-tuned. Sadly, if our trust has been betrayed to extreme degrees or too many times, we are likely to look suspiciously at any new person in our lives and tend to keep others at a safe distance.

A major reason people are hesitant to set boundaries is that they view them as barriers or tools used to keep people at arm's length. Contrary to that notion, when you form a clear boundary you are in fact inviting them in, on your terms. By sharing your values with that person, you are giving them a tool to nurture a relationship with you. This creates a safe space for you to be open and vulnerable with each other, which is essential for any relationship to flourish. Boundaries are not about shutting people out at all; they are an essential part of strong relationships.

The irony of trust lies in its necessity. To form those deep, enriching connections with others we have to have trust. Yet, it's the one thing that can hurt us the most if it comes to be betrayed. So, how do we motivate ourselves to trust someone after getting burned?

Do It for You!

There's one crucial thing we all must accept: living with a constant guard up, neck-deep in trust issues, is a much more boring life to endure than one that's filled with a genuine openness and some occasional heartbreaks.

Forgiveness and trust have some key commonalities. We tend to think of these actions as something we give to others who we deem worthy or deserving of them. Interestingly enough, trust and forgiveness have more to do with ourselves and our inner peace. Neither is emotionally easy and both make us feel vulnerable to our core. It's not easy to trust again after a betrayal, nor is it always palatable to forgive someone who has caused deep pain.

"To forgive is to set a prisoner free and discover that the prisoner was you," said Lewis B. Smedes, and he could not have put it better. Of course, choosing to trust again and forgiving one's past betrayals are not synonymous, but they are certainly correlated. Through forgiveness, you tell yourself it's okay to finally let go of that hurt. It could be as simple as you needing to forgive yourself for trusting someone that ultimately hurt you. If you aren't ready to forgive another person for something they did, at least be willing to liberate yourself from the burden of pain it caused. It is about finding acceptance for what happened, leaving history in the past, and allowing yourself to move on.

The Power of Being Vulnerable

Entertainment media and even our everyday interactions prove that society at large still portrays vulnerability as a weakness. Many of us are taught to keep our vulnerabilities hidden away so as not to be taken advantage of. Because of the possibility of rejection or failure, we tend to perceive vulnerability as a risky endeavor. Any time we make ourselves vulnerable, we are taking the risk of an intense emotional response due to the higher stakes involved. However, if no one ever introduced a wild idea that was sure to be shot down, we wouldn't have achieved any of the innovations that make modern life so comfortable.

I used to consult with an individual named Ashley. She prided herself on being outspoken and had earned the respect of her colleagues, but had become stuck in a cycle of limiting herself after some recent ideas had been brushed off. Ashley displayed vulnerability by proposing creative ideas and felt defeated when they were disregarded by her team. Her knee-jerk reaction was to muzzle herself and support an idea proposed by a teammate instead.

I wanted to delve deeper into Ashley's mindset so I asked her what might have been lackluster about her proposals. Were they impractical? Did they fail to address the team's goal? What roadblocks had she overlooked that would derail her plan? Why might her colleagues have disregarded the ideas in question? Through our conversations, it became clear that Ashley had a big-picture idea but had been watering it down to conform with the expected reaction from her team. She didn't want to ruffle any feathers or dream too big. Essentially, Ashley - the poster child of displaying vulnerability - was still limiting herself. We concluded that her proposals were solid and, rather than muzzling herself, Ashley needed to become *more* vulnerable and communicate her full proposal. She was treating her vulnerability as a weakness, but it was clear to me that her fearlessness to speak up was a trait her colleagues admired about her and it had allowed her to grow to this point in her career.

Ashley strutted into our next meeting looking victorious. She had made peace with her recent defeat and reintroduced her proposal, this time confidently presenting the full picture and elaborating on the details that would give the proposal wings to fly. She was praised for her outside-the-box approach and the team agreed to move forward with the first phase of her plan.

Being vulnerable isn't a sign of weakness, it is a sign of courage and lies at the basis of authentic connections. Ironically, it's only when we're able to establish healthy boundaries that we can fully appreciate the positive sides of vulnerability.

The Side-effects of Unhealthy Boundaries

We've discussed some of the positive effects of setting boundaries, but what happens when we *don't* set them? What are the side effects?

Generally, having poor boundaries will lead to resentment, anger, and burnout. The consequences of not setting healthy boundaries often include stress, feeling overwhelmed, financial problems, wasted time, and relationship issues, all of which have a great impact on our well-being.

Many people who are suffering from a lack of boundaries in their relationships don't even recognize why they feel so bad. I know too many people who have become victims of this. Their time was exploited, their personal belongings and safety were violated, and oftentimes their emotional state was not even considered. They knew they felt awful, but they didn't know *why*.

When your boundaries are either too loose or too rigid, your needs go unmet. This can lead to dissatisfaction and ultimately to anxiety, losing touch with yourself, and even depression. People with boundaries that are too loose often report difficulty identifying their own emotions and needs. Let's say you are overly agreeable and frequently suppress your own opinions in deference to the opinions of others. There reaches a point where you may lose sight of the line that separates your authentic self from the mask you put on to relate with the people in your life. Becoming over-involved in other people's lives, perfectionism, people-pleasing, and taking on excessive amounts of commitments are all common symptoms pointing to a lack of healthy boundaries.

Boundaries that are too rigid often come from a fear of losing your freedom and independence, which leads to feelings of emptiness and loneliness. Boundaries that are too rigid stem from the paradoxical interplay between a desire for connection and the dread of intimacy. Rigid boundaries safeguard your vulnerability, keeping it locked away.

In our journey toward setting healthy boundaries, it is important to make sure our current (and future) boundaries are not too loose and not too rigid.

Recognizing Unhealthy Boundaries

Let's look at some situations people with poor boundaries find themselves in:

- *Feeling disrespected in your relationships.* A person who makes you feel disrespected is not necessarily doing so out of hatred—more often than not, they do not recognize how their actions are making you feel. If your husband thinks you don't have an issue with him leaving dirty dishes on the counter, he will continue to do so.

- *Feeling unsafe in your relationships.* A person's behavior should never trigger a sense of danger within you. Likewise, you should not feel the relationship is at stake if you refuse to go along with someone's demands. Feeling safe speaks not just to physical danger, but your emotional stability and well-being should not be threatened either.

- *Emotions of jealousy and envy.* If you are with someone who is naturally flirty, you might understand what I'm talking about. Let's say your partner is a flirt but you are well aware that they have no intention of betraying your relationship. They love you, but their flirtatiousness gets the best of them. Even if you know your partner is like this, you might find this style of communication troubling. By not speaking up, you give your partner space to continue flirting with others, and you will continue to suffer in silence. Which sounds harder: enduring mind-numbing jealousy every time the two of you go out or having one potentially awkward, yet honest conversation?

- *Struggle to be there for others in a meaningful way.* When you are expected to give an inordinate amount of your time to a few people in your life, how will you be able to be there for others? Your automatic, unconscious response to someone wanting to spend time with you might be a sense of dread. You likely feel spread too thin and struggle to be emotionally present in many of your relationships. It is difficult to form connections founded on mutual respect.

- *Lower self-esteem.* Not only does your self-esteem suffer when you are being treated with less respect than you deserve, but this can be augmented by the fact that you are suppressing your authenticity. If you stop being able to be happy in certain relationships, you often have to fake it. For example, you may find yourself constantly going along with the unusual demands of a friend or relative, eventually convincing yourself it makes you happy to appease them. This lack of genuineness often makes people start to dislike themselves, seeing as they are, in essence, not living out their truth.

- *Feeling numb.* Numbness is a consequence of poor boundaries that tends to occur after a long period of time. The longer you go without setting boundaries, the less likely you are to set them. We start losing touch with what we want and need, feel empty, and don't know who we are anymore. It's a feeling of being so deep in the trenches you may as well not bother climbing out.

Key Takeaways

- You cannot have healthy relationships unless you have a healthy trust level—too little or too much of it can cause your boundaries to be either too rigid or too loose.

- Do not let your painful experiences in the past hold control over your present and future relationships.
- Willingness to express vulnerability is essential to forming strong bonds.
- Resentment, anger, and feeling overwhelmed are some key indicators that firmer boundaries need to be applied.

Chapter 3
What's Needed for Boundaries?

Boundaries protect the things that are of value to you. They keep you in alignment with what you have decided you want in life. That means the key to good boundaries is knowing what you want.

— Adelyn Birch

Setting boundaries is difficult! I get it. In fact, I've *lived* it. But if we don't establish boundaries, other people won't know how to interact with us. We'll end up feeling disrespected and misunderstood. On top of that, we may start to resent others when we're unable to recognize our own boundaries.

Let's take a quick look at an example: You are living with your romantic partner who you've been with for several years now. The honeymoon phase is over, you are both very comfortable in each other's presence and you consider your relationship to be a loving one overall. You both work full-time jobs with somewhat different schedules, contributing pretty equally to your household's finances. Now, imagine that you are beginning to notice your counterpart is doing far less around the house than you. Let's say they end work at four in the afternoon, but you're done at nine. You regularly come home after a long day at work and find your partner sitting amongst a pile of unfolded laundry, or a stack of dirty dishes from breakfast remains in the sink. You're exhausted from your day and would rather not initiate a conversation about this, so you do these chores yourself.

This scenario tends to set off little red flags for most people because we are primed to expect a degree of reciprocity in our relationships. This feeling of disappointment and being let down by your partner may challenge your sense of self-worth. When someone is not pulling their weight with the simple things, you may question their ability to meaningfully contribute to the relationship when it matters most.

Now, do you think this person is leaving chores for you out of malice or ill intent? I doubt the answer is yes, however it is more important to first examine your reaction to the emotions that come about when someone lets you down. Beyond assigning an assumed reason for the bad behavior, how does it make you feel? Are there larger aspects of the relationship that this small household chore might call into question? Get clear on what it is about the neglected chores that sets you off. It is exactly these things that need to be addressed when you confront your partner with the issue.

You see, if this is a healthy relationship, you will probably have to go through a conversation or two to set this boundary straight. Boundaries are not a form of harsh ultimatums nor are they meant to sour the vibe between two people. They are simply a definition of your limits, encouraging others to keep them in mind.

Instead of starting a conversation about your partner not pulling their weight, a more effective approach would sound more like "Honey, when you do x, it makes me feel y". Expressing those feelings calls on you to be vulnerable, which signals that you care enough to solve the issue rather than revert to anger or the blame game. By getting better at addressing the root cause of the problem at hand you will likely have a more productive outcome.

Getting Clear on Your Why

Goals and vision are vital for growth in life, career, and relationships. Without them, we let life happen to us and give up our power and control to the winds of fate. What if I told you that you can have everything you need in life?

Now, don't get me wrong, obviously we can't control everything in life. Regaining your power has everything to do with understanding what you *can* and what you *cannot* control. And let me tell you one thing: the only thing you have control over is yourself. If you're unhappy about certain aspects of your life, it might be time to take back control. A good starting point is thinking about your vision and goals.

Sometimes used interchangeably, goals and vision are two separate, co-existing concepts. Your vision is your why. It provides direction and gives you the brush to paint the picture of a future you desire. Your vision is a powerful source of motivation. Once you've got a clear image of what your ideal future looks like, your goals are the practical steps that get you there.

Now, what do your goals and vision have to do with boundaries? Boundaries can serve as a powerful tool for achieving your goals and realizing your vision. Without clear boundaries, we move away from what we actually want and sometimes even forget what it was to begin with. Without a clear vision of what we want out of life, our need for boundaries might not be so apparent, since we are not prioritizing our own goals. We get so caught up in our daily lives and before we know it, years have gone by. People who never become fully aware of their true desires tend to feel generally dissatisfied in life without recognizing exactly why or how to fix it.

On the other hand, having clearly defined goals can make it easier to set boundaries. Once you've got your vision and the steps that will get you closer to it, you might find it easier to say 'no' to the people or commitments that do not serve you.

To help you on your way to imagining your vision you can use the exercise below. This is one of my favorite exercises because you can go all out on this one. I want to invite you to dream big and make it as specific as possible.

Exercise 1: Visualize your Ideal Future

Follow the next steps to the best of your abilities and you will maximize the potential effects that this practice has:

1. Treat this exercise like a meditation—sit in a calm environment, get comfortable, and start awakening

your powerful imagination. You can even put on some meditation music if you want.

2. For this exercise, you can either focus on your whole life or a certain aspect of it (e.g., your relationships, work, money, health, etc.)

3. Close your eyes and take a few deep breaths until you feel your body and mind calming down. Focus on your breathing and *feel* the weight of gravity pulling you down into a deeper state of relaxation.

4. When you feel completely calm, I want you to start imagining your dream life (or an aspect of your dream life). What does this future look like? What are you doing? What do you feel like? What kind of a job do you have? How are your relationships? Who surrounds you? Who are you spending your time with? Where do you live? What does this environment look like? What do you look like? Try to imagine this future life in as much detail as possible. To solidify this, you can do this from both your point of view and an external point of view.

5. When you have a clear picture try to dig into your physical and emotional state. What does your body feel like? Any specific physical sensations? Do you feel proud? Giddy? Happy? Excited? Whatever you expect it to be, try to manufacture it in your state of visualization—truly *feel* that moment as if it's already happening.

6. Slowly bring your awareness back to the room around you and open your eyes.

When you're done with this exercise, I want you to write down your experience in detail. Look at the questions from the exercise and try to answer them. Hopefully, this was a beautiful experience that will stick with you for a long time. You can do this exercise as often as you want. Don't lose sight of the dream life you've imagined. Repeat this exercise often and focus on the aspects that make you happiest, honing in on your priorities. The more time you allow yourself to spend refining your vision, the easier it will be to determine what kind of goals you'll need to get there.

Exercise 2: Goal setting

Now that you have a clear vision I want you to pick an area of your dream life and start thinking about actionable goals to realize your vision.

The following questions can help you to make your goals more distinct and clearer:

- What is your goal? Describe it in one sentence.
- Why do you desire to achieve this goal? Are your intentions coming from a place of true fulfillment or rather gratification of vain desire?
- How do you believe you will feel and continue to live once your goal has been achieved?
- What are the biggest obstacles standing between you and this goal?
- Why haven't you started working toward this goal earlier? Be honest: Was it circumstance or something else (fear/intimidation/lack of discipline etc.)?
- Are you able to achieve this goal on your own or should you plan on seeking assistance from others?

- Is there anyone you look up to in terms of this goal? And why? Can you copy some of their habits/character traits?
- Do you have a relatively mapped-out idea of the steps you must take to achieve this goal?

Answering these questions not only grounds your belief that achieving this goal is truly valuable to your life, but also helps you to better communicate your desires and needs to achieve that goal.

If you ever feel yourself being pulled away from these goals by others, thinking of this exercise will help you to put out a more compelling case, giving the other person a better reason to attend to you. When you have a clear picture of what you want and don't want, it won't be as easy for people to derail you from it.

An Uncomfortable Truth

Annie Dillard once said: "How we spend our days is how we spend our lives." This quote has always resonated with me because it's such an obvious statement, but at the same time has a deeper meaning. As much as we'd like to, we can't change our lives in a day or a week. Change happens as a result of small adjustments on a day-to-day basis. Even the most driven people who fully embrace change frequently run into roadblocks that make their transformation far more challenging than originally expected.

We're often quite capable of envisioning our dream life and are actually quite good at setting goals. Who doesn't like to set a goal about earning more money? Or living a healthier life? The problem with keeping and achieving goals often has to do with facing one simple, but uncomfortable truth: if you want to change the world around you, it is *you* who needs to change. We would love to take control over our surroundings, circumstances, and other people, but the reality is that we can only control ourselves.

Obviously "changing yourself" is not as easy as it sounds. Believe me, this is my life's work. I know how hard it is to change yourself. But I'm seeing that it is possible, every single day, over and over again. With clearly defined goals and healthy boundaries in place, I have no doubt you can do the same.

Key Takeaways

- Boundaries are not about telling other people what to do, they're about validating your feelings and giving them space at the table
- By having a clear vision and setting practical goals we can create lasting change
- Boundaries help us to protect our vision and goals just as our goals help us to define clear boundaries
- Change happens in small increments and comes from within

Chapter 4
Why it's Hard to Set Boundaries

When you say 'yes' to others, make sure you're not saying 'no' to yourself.

— Paulo Coelho

As social creatures, we have a primal need to belong to a community and form strong bonds of attachment with others. In the past, this was a matter of life or death. Early humans depended on collaboration, sharing knowledge, and pooling resources to grow in population. While the stakes are considerably lower today, imagine if you woke up tomorrow and your closest friend or romantic partner decided never speak to you again. This development would likely be devastating. You would feel crushed for losing someone that means so much to you. This need for closeness frequently causes us to disregard our personal boundaries and, in doing so, we end up dissatisfied.

The Lie of Selfishness

There's a reason why so many of us identify as people-pleasers. We are told that doing things for others is honorable and doing things for ourselves is not. The first half of that message is indeed correct—doing things for others is a good thing and expresses our compassion for them. However, for various reasons, many of us struggle with the feeling that being kind to ourselves is a form of vanity.

Let's make one thing clear: putting yourself first is *not* selfish. There's a saying I particularly like regarding this that goes "if you don't fill your gas tank, you can't carry passengers." You can't be expected to take care of others when you aren't taking care of yourself. I have many clients who work 60+ hours per week, still help their parents out around the house, and manage to raise a family while juggling their social life. Whenever we talk about self-care, they often tell me that it's just another item on their to-do list. One of my clients once said: "Taking a moment for myself feels more like a burden than something that makes me happy. I just don't have the time for it."

But when you are *always* attending to others, you are running on fumes. If your car runs out of gas, you don't keep slamming on the gas pedal, expecting it to move. You face the fact that you have to refuel it. Yet, you might struggle to apply the same strategy to yourself. You could be exhausted before you even step out of bed, yet if your phone rings with an urgent request from a coworker, your mouth will be saying 'sure' before your head has even realized what it signed up for.

I'll reiterate this: by saying 'no' to others, you're saying 'yes' to yourself. But how often do you actually do that? Taking some time for yourself simply ensures that you give the same amount of care that you show to others to yourself. Anyone who doesn't let you do that is not a friend of yours and they will not be getting your best.

Selfishness is when someone is concerned solely with their own happiness and well-being and does not care about others. Kindly telling someone you would prefer to stay in and recharge rather than help them with a project on your day off is far from selfish. It's time to change the narrative and take back your power to determine the things you dedicate your time and energy to.

In my journey to set healthy boundaries I learned a very important lesson. The only people who reacted negatively when I finally set firm boundaries were the ones who had benefited from trampling over mine for many years. As I'm sure many others can relate, one of my strongest barriers was the idea that people close to me would find my new determination selfish or rude. I knew this feeling came from a place of insecurity, but I couldn't shake it off until I understood one important concept. It suddenly clicked. If people around me are angry because I can't commit to helping them at the expense of my own obligations, they don't respect my time. Or if they are hurt by the fact I can no longer lend them money because I need it myself, they do not respect my financial well-being.

The People-Pleasing Habit

In extreme cases, people-pleasing can be associated with a personality trait known as *sociotropy,* or being overly concerned with pleasing others to sustain relationships. Someone with sociotropy will overvalue social acceptance to the point they struggle with the possibility of a negative outcome. They feel as if they are obligated to change their approach to the relationship or put in a greater effort to produce a positive final result. If their partner comes home in a bad mood due to something that occurred at work, simply comforting their partner would not feel like enough. They would have to do anything in their power to make their partner feel better and try to 'fix' the situation. This type of person will go to extreme lengths to make their partner feel better and are so fixated on solving the problem they may become misguided in their approach. But, thinking that their partner's mood at the end of the day is entirely dependent on their actions is not only damaging but completely unrealistic.

A person with sociotropy also tends to place the well-being of others above their own happiness and independence. They will sacrifice their autonomy, all of their time, a lot of their money, and other aspects of their independence in an attempt to maintain closeness in the relationship. Consequently, they are deeply affected by a relationship ending or even some conflict arising within it. It's probably obvious at this point that someone with sociotropy struggles to lead a happy life for themselves and often gives up self-respect and their independence for something that is ultimately far beyond their control.

Not nearly all people-pleasers suffer from sociotropy, though it bears mentioning as the extremes to which people-pleasing can go. For example, one of the biggest characteristics of a people-pleaser is putting someone else's happiness above your own well-being. People-pleasing is a harmful trait and many of us find ourselves somewhere on the spectrum.

So, *why* is it that people-pleasing is so common? In reality, there are many possible causes, including:

- Trauma, especially from childhood or past relationships
- Being upheld to unrealistically high expectations by your family and feeling as if you were never enough
- Only being granted attention and care from those around you if you do as they say
- Feeling unseen by those you care about as if your needs are not as important as their expectations
- You want the person you are trying to please to be indebted to you
- You are afraid of the relationship ending if you don't adhere to the other person's every requirement

People-pleasing is inherently contradictory to the concept of setting boundaries. Why? Because the former is done solely for your counterpart and the latter is done for *your* benefit. People who cannot kick their people-pleasing habit will have a hard time motivating themselves to set boundaries and accepting the possibility of introducing conflict to a relationship.

Are you a people-pleaser? Even if you say no, perhaps you might still exhibit some aspects of this habit. Here are 10 signs that you might be somewhat of a people-pleaser (Morin, 2017):

1. You pretend to agree with people's opinions even if you do not.
2. You feel a strong sense of responsibility for other people's emotions.
3. You apologize too often—almost habitually.
4. You feel exhausted with your schedule, especially if it is filled to the brim with activities you feel pressured to join in on but do not enjoy.
5. You struggle to say 'no'.
6. You can't handle it when someone close to you is upset with you.
7. You often take on the personalities or behaviors of those around you.
8. You seek constant validation and reassurance to believe someone likes you.
9. You would do anything to prevent a conflict with someone.
10. You keep it to yourself if you are upset and suppress negative emotions

Being a people-pleaser is nothing to be ashamed of. The concept of social conformity affects all of us and has been the topic of study for many sociologists and psychologists for decades.

As has been a recurring theme throughout the past several chapters, we are relatively easily influenced by those around us. In fact, we are affected even by those who might be physically distant, yet their influence reigns over us.

The process of kicking the pesky habit of people-pleasing is not an overnight change. It is a process of reprogramming not only how you view others, but how you view yourself as well. Distancing yourself from some people-pleasing habits will have some overlap with a technique that is familiar to us all: setting goals and prioritizing your own life. When we set goals for ourselves and visualize a desirable outcome, we remind ourselves that the happiness of those around us is not the defining component of *our* happiness. When we start prioritizing ourselves, we are recovering from that habit of only ever pleasing others. Furthermore, it opens our eyes to the undeniable fact that we cannot possibly build up to our future achievements if we spend our present solely worried about others who do not reciprocate this energy. Once we are clear on our desires, we can fully commit to them by being radically honest. Yes, keeping them to ourselves protects us from possible conflict in the short run, but by always being truthful we will reap the benefits in the mid to long-term.

Other than reminding ourselves of our desires and goals, we could also (Cherry, 2021):

- Start small. When training to be able to stand up for ourselves, we can start practicing on things that hold little significance. For example, politely say no to a small request that will barely affect the other person; or you could voice your opinion to someone even if they have a different point of view on something. You could even try to say 'no' through a text or email and then work your way up to telling people 'no' in person.
- Practice positive and uplifting self-talk. We are constantly talking to ourselves and about ourselves, even if we don't notice or admit it. What we say is very important. So, start watching and noticing your thoughts about yourself: Do you put

yourself down? Do you justify the poor treatment you are offered by others? If so, start shifting your self-talk from "I owe this person my time" to something like "I am owed the autonomy to spend my time how I wish."

- Don't immediately say yes to requests. If someone asks you for yet another favor, don't say yes right at that moment, even if you have to bite your tongue. Instead, say something along the lines of "I'm not sure at the moment, but let me get back to you." By saying this, you are not only preventing yourself from agreeing to something prematurely but it might be easier for you to decline their favor when you're not in the heat of the moment. Before you give them your final answer, you have the time to evaluate whether you can (or should) commit to it.

- Assess if the person is asking or expecting too much of you. If someone is asking you for something, stop and think about their pattern of behavior. How often do they ask you for something? Is their request reasonable? Are they someone who reciprocates your efforts and helps you out from time to time? Will they have a negative or nasty reaction if you were to decline (i.e. do they feel entitled to your time and efforts)?

- Remind yourself that relationships of all kinds require reciprocation. If a friend, for example, only takes and takes without giving you anything back, they are flat-out being a bad friend. Perhaps talking to them and setting some boundaries will help them adjust their behavior.

When you are just starting out in your recovery from people-pleasing, you might be tempted to cut some corners to make the process easier for yourself and I don't blame you! There is no shame in this—as long as you are trying and making some progress, you are already taking one step toward the new you.

A lot of people find that they need to justify all of their answers to a fault. This can look like a rambling, detailed explanation as to *why* they are saying no to a particular request. I understand why this might be tempting for someone who is used to always saying yes, but unfortunately, when you do this, you continue to invalidate yourself. By overly explaining why you are declining a request, you communicate that you can't justify your reasons for doing so. The bottom line is that we do not need to justify our answer to someone's request. We can just say no, simply because we feel like it.

Clouded by Society

Going back to our human need for belonging, social norms and expectations weigh heavily on how we view boundaries and the values we prioritize. Although we are living through a period of rapid social change, we continue to be strongly encouraged to behave and relate to others in specific ways that are rewarded by the society we belong to. Therefore it is important to examine how susceptible we are to limiting our individuality in an effort to fit in.

My grandmother was a great example of someone who was successfully convinced by society that she owed it all to my grandfather. Now, to be clear, he was a great man, but the norms society instilled in both of their heads hovered over them their entire lives, well into the 21st century. She moved in with him straight from her parent's house and became a stay-at-home wife the moment they got married. Throughout my entire childhood, she told me all about the 'lovely' things she got to do while at home. She said she was perfectly satisfied taking care of the house and turning it into a home. Eventually, they had four children, and her time became occupied with them. My grandfather worked and was the traditional breadwinner.

As I became older, I started to see the cracks in their stories and the doubt behind their smiles. When I was in my twenties, my grandmother and I had a heartfelt conversation in which she encouraged me to take advantage of all the opportunities presented to me while expressing some regrets from her past. She told me about her passion for science and her fascination with the stars. Deep down she wanted to be an astronomer but never even got the chance to learn about such a subject. It was the only time she ever shared this truth about her desires, and it pained me to hear her lament the missed opportunities in her life. Shortly after she passed away, my grandfather also spoke more openly about how the expectations of his time had influenced his choices. He was always such a powerful, artsy inspiration in my life. He was a fantastic painter when he eventually retired and even started learning the piano when he was 68 years old. He too had wanted to live a life that was different from the one he had led. One filled with art instead of machines in an industrial factory. I believe they were genuinely happy at the end of their lives, but it was striking to hear them both refer to society-induced limitations being among their life's greatest regrets.

It's easier said than done to live a life untethered by others and unchained from social constructs. But seeing how our independent desires are formed and influenced by culture and society is a good first step.

Key Takeaways

- While helping others is certainly a good trait, it becomes draining if others' needs become prioritized over your own.
- Sociotropy is a trait closely related to people-pleasing, causing someone to be overly invested in making others happy.
- People-pleasing causes someone to avoid conflict and can prevent them from setting boundaries.
- Society has a strong influence over our views of relationships and our role in them.

Chapter 5
Unearthing Your Self-Worth

Strong people have a strong sense of self-worth and self-awareness; they don't need the approval of others.

— Roy T. Bennett

There is a reason why so much material regarding boundary-setting is directly correlated with how confident we are in ourselves. Think of someone confident, do you imagine them letting others walk all over them? Do they agree to things they don't want to do and regret not doing what they wanted? Or are they able to casually say 'no' in a way that makes others respect their response without demanding an explanation?

One fool-proof way of checking if someone respects you or not is how they respond to your 'no.' If they poke holes in it, demand to know every little detail about why you are choosing to say 'no', or attempt to turn your 'no' into a 'yes', it could indicate they don't respect you or your time. Being made to feel obligated to justify your answer is an indication the other person won't respect your answer unless their ego deems it valid. To change this, we need to learn how to stand our ground. To confront another's *ego,* we benefit from understanding ourselves and augmenting our confidence and self-esteem.

It is important to note the key difference between ego and self-esteem. Self-esteem is one's *confidence* in their own capabilities and skills. It comes from within. Ego, however, is the *opinion* a person has of themself and is based on external validation. Ego says more about how important one feels around others whereas self-esteem is a measure of self-respect.

Let's take a difficult job interview as an example. A person with low self-esteem will be bombarded with doubt leading up to the said interview. They might procrastinate out of fear, feel extremely anxious, or even give up before trying. Someone with healthy self-esteem is excited about such a challenge with a potential reward. They will approach it differently: They will grab the tools and resources they need and start preparing to give their best. They believe they deserve to give this interview their best shot because they have what it takes to get the job.

A person with an inflated ego could be presumptuous and go into the interview assuming they will automatically move to the next round simply because they deserve this job. An inflated sense of self-importance and entitlement guides this belief rather than authentic confidence in their abilities or self-worth. They might not even prepare for the interview or plan to outsmart or manipulate the interviewers.

A particularly egotistical person will likely set unequal boundaries. They will set boundaries that only benefit them while exploiting others. Oftentimes, these attempts are manipulative in nature. For example, they might say "I feel neglected if you don't spend every free night with me. I should be your priority and I feel like you spending time with your friends is disrespectful to our relationship." Hopefully, this doesn't sound familiar to any of you, but it happens more often than one might think.

Oddly enough, society tends to reward ego-fueled achievements, so we're destined to have our boundaries challenged by a few inflated egos throughout our journey of life. The best way to handle toxic egotistical behavior rests in a defined sense of self-worth. We'll be discussing techniques to examine our self-esteem in the next section. These exercises should make you more comfortable in your power, opening the door to becoming more assertive when needed.

Self-Worth Theory

The way people view themselves is such a complex thing to understand, there are entire branches of psychology dedicated to figuring it out. Isn't that ironic? One of the hardest things for us to understand in life is ourselves. The self-worth theory is a psychological theory that states the ultimate goal in people's lives is finding self-worth through self-acceptance and achievement (Ackerman, 2018).

The theory goes on to describe that there are four key components that make up the self-worth model:

- Ability
- Effort
- Performance
- Self-worth

The first three bullet points interplay with each other to make up your self-worth. If you have strong abilities and put in enough effort, your performance will likely be exceptional. When your performance is good, your self-worth will be as well.

While this theory is a decent representation of many people's mentalities, it doesn't cover the entire truth. Yes, our achievements play a massive role in the way we view ourselves and how much we think we are worth. However, if our self-worth is *entirely* rooted in achievement, we risk losing it at the first sign of failure. Life isn't linear—we will have good days, bad days, great days, and awful days. If we attach our worth to these ever-changing conditions, we give up stability.

The Determinants

Here are some good questions to ask yourself: What makes you feel good about yourself? What makes you feel bad about yourself? And what factors can you identify that determine how much worth you see in yourself?

Everyone's answers will be different, but research has found that some factors tend to generally overlap. Those commonly mentioned factors can be categorized as follows (Ackerman, 2018):

- Appearance

- Net worth and finances
- Our social network
- Our career success
- Achievements

Getting into college, being accepted for a job or a promotion, trying to appear a certain way to others; our lives are filled with competition. It's a universal trait for us to feel good when we manage to do something a little better than others. It proves our ability to meaningfully contribute to society, nurturing our need for belonging. This is naturally ingrained in most of us, but it doesn't necessarily serve us in regard to our self-worth. We have to learn that our worth runs so much deeper than our achievements. You are worthy simply because you exist, nothing more. Self-worth should come from a place of unconditional love. Instead of getting caught up in chasing money, status and popularity we should work on identifying and challenging our critical inner voice. Fully commit to treating yourself with kindness, tolerance, generosity, and compassion.

Seeing Neutrality

My niece is someone I'm very close to in this life. She's a wonderful young woman, and she and I get along very well. In her teens, however, she began to struggle with her self-esteem and adopted quite an unhealthy self-image. She tried for years to find her confidence but her high school years were, simply put, hellish.

She focused on every superficial quality imaginable. Her lack of wealth was embarrassing, her body was ugly and she felt inferior to her peers.

My niece is a go-getter and she set out to tackle these perceived shortcomings with a vengeance. I had to give it to her, even if I disagreed with her approach. She was able to achieve the appearance of a lifestyle she wanted via social media channels and she felt more confident because of it. She had confronted her insecurities by achieving an image of superiority - being the best, more beautiful, more successful than her peers. But as soon as she got negative feedback, the fragility of her meticulously built house of cards became apparent and her self-esteem took a nosedive.

So I introduced her to a new approach: the rule of neutrality. The rule of neutrality is simply the concept of seeing yourself as neither good nor bad. If you hate the way you look today, you don't have to convince yourself you're beautiful. Instead, start telling yourself you're simply in a body—its beauty is subjective, and you have no obligation to see yourself as a walking god or goddess; your body's beauty or lack thereof is not a determinant of your worth. No one of us is truly, objectively, more beautiful than anyone else.

I told my niece to apply this to all the areas she lacked confidence in. She doesn't need to think she's a genius, but she also doesn't need to tell herself she is unintelligent; she doesn't have to think her clothes are runway-worthy, but she shouldn't see them as rags either. After all, these are egotistical desires and her authentic worth was unattached to any of these aspects. It wasn't easy and it took her some years, but eventually, she became comfortable with neutrality. She was able to look at other girls and say "yes, she has fashionable clothes and a body that wears them well, but I wear my style in my own way."

It was only after she accepted the fact that there will always be something or someone better, she started to transition into a more confident woman. Her clothes served their purpose, her body was doing everything it was supposed to, the amount of money she had was nobody's business. With the gratitude she found through the rule of neutrality, she was able to shift toward a more positive mindset and higher self-esteem.

I would invite you to try it yourself. Treat neutrality as the foundation on which your future confidence and self-esteem will be based. See yourself as neutral: you are simply you. Feel the balance within your life, push away the superficial labels. Yes, there are aspects of your life that can be improved but that is no reason to hate them as they are right now.

Understanding Potential

As you probably noticed in my earlier example about self-esteem versus ego, someone with healthy self-esteem holds confidence in the things they believe they are capable of. Yes, their self-esteem is probably based on their successes from the past, but even with the fluctuations of successes and failures, they continue to believe that they will be just as capable to meet future challenges.

People who have good self-esteem generally have at least a basic sense of their skills and what they are good at or can become good at. Now, to truly know your capabilities and inclinations you might require some in-depth soul-searching but getting to know yourself is worth it in the long run.

"But, what if I'm not particularly good at anything? Will I not be able to develop my self-esteem?" A valid question considering what we just discussed, but the answer is a resounding 'yes'. First of all, there is always some area in your life where you excel. Perhaps you don't place a particularly high value on that skill or talent, but I refuse to believe there is anyone on this earth that does not excel in one thing or another, no matter how trivial it may seem. Another important thing to understand is that our abilities are dynamic, not static. This is part of the larger concept of a growth mindset versus a fixed mindset. In short, a growth mindset is when a person believes they can become good at new things, learn additional skills, and improve upon existing ones. A fixed mindset is at the opposite end of that spectrum and is present when a person thinks their skills are determined by chance and they are not capable of changing their potency.

You don't have to be a wunderkind at something to develop your self-esteem. However, you must strive toward something and believe in yourself. Allow yourself to acknowledge the areas where you excel. Try to see the skills or character traits you possess as your small contribution to the world around you. Give that contribution some validation and take ownership. There are billions of us on this earth and we all have but a tiny part to play in the human story. Once you're able to accept that you possess unique skills or character traits that make your contribution unique, it is easier to believe you are worthy of achieving greater things. Accept what you're already good at, validate the notion that you are capable of achieving great things and let that fuel your ability to develop new skills as well.

If this all sounds a bit ambiguous, try doing the visualization technique we went over in chapter 3. Identify a goal that takes you just one step closer to a vision that makes you happiest, and go for it.

Accepting Compliments

Whenever I mention that accepting compliments is directly tied to a person's ability to set solid boundaries, people get confused. Soon, the correlation will make sense.

There are four common reasons why a person might struggle to accept the compliments they are given (Morin, 2016):

1. **Low self-esteem.** Hey, we just talked about that! Low self-esteem isn't just not believing in yourself, but it's also a refusal to accept that *others* can believe in you. In other words, you have so little faith in yourself that you can't fathom the idea that others have faith in you. For example, if you think you have awful taste in style, it is almost jarring to hear someone compliment your outfit— so much so that it is unbelievable to you.

2. **Different self-image.** Even without low self-esteem, we struggle to wrap our heads around the fact that people view us differently from how we view ourselves. Furthermore, each person views us a bit differently than the next. This inconsistency between how we are told we are viewed compared to how we view ourselves is often referred to as cognitive dissonance. When a person compliments us on a trait we perceive as a flaw, we will struggle

to accept it. A compliment like that will make you either reconsider your self-image or question the other person's honesty.

3. **Your bar is lower than theirs.** Oftentimes, people who cannot accept compliments simply diminish their successes and skills. They tend to shy away from others' expectations if they appear to be too big. To someone like this, a compliment like "you're such a hard worker," might trigger anxiety because they don't want to disappoint when they don't live up to their expectations.

4. **You want to stay humble.** This is a trait that is shared by most people. Even those that don't struggle to accept compliments do struggle with finding a balanced response to them. If we were to agree with the person giving a compliment, we often view ourselves as coming off cocky. "You are such a talented student," is hard to follow with "yes, I agree." So, to avoid reacting in a potentially arrogant manner, we often resort to disagreeing with the compliment altogether. Instead, the proper solution to this problem would be to thank the person for the compliment without agreeing or disagreeing with it.

In full transparency, accepting compliments will continue to be difficult as long as your self-esteem and self-worth are below healthy levels. Therefore, you must start applying the rule of neutrality, increase your self-esteem, and then start to accept compliments as they were meant to be received.

The ability to accept compliments is important for someone trying to set boundaries. Accepting a compliment and forming a boundary are both manifestations of how we interact with others and allow outsiders to view us. When we properly acknowledge a compliment and receive it well, we are allowing that person to view us in a positive light and accept that we are worthy of praise. When communicating our boundaries, we are enforcing a similar concept. We are laying out a framework that governs how a person can interact with us while acknowledging that our autonomy, time, and mental health is worth preserving. One action is more passive—receiving a compliment—and the other occurs only through applied action—setting boundaries.

If we don't allow ourselves to accept compliments, we are furthering the idea that we mean very little to others. When we start believing compliments and accepting them, we are solidifying the idea that we are worthy of respect. The more we communicate to the world that we are worthy of respect, the easier it becomes to set healthy boundaries.

Direct Action

The way we view ourselves largely shapes the type of life we have. Perspective is everything, truly. It's easier said than done, but a simple shift in mindset is sometimes enough to get a glimpse of the light at the end of the tunnel. There are people who are naturally predisposed toward a more optimistic outlook on their life just as there are people who tend to view things in a more negative light. In some instances, perspective can be heavily skewed by common mental health issues such as depression or anxiety, but more often it is simply a case of a nasty habit.

Are there times when you feel negativity taking over in your own thoughts? Here's a list of a few things you can start doing today to become a more positive person. Seeing the world and your life in a more positive light can work wonders on improving your self-esteem:

- **Practice being more grateful.** Easy, right? Well, I'm giving you some homework. Take out a journal and list five things you are grateful for today. Make it a new habit to do this every day. By bringing our conscious attention to what we are happy to have in our lives, we balance out our perception of the negatives. You can even start improving your self-esteem by writing things about yourself you are grateful for—even the smallest things will do!

- **Evaluate your skills.** There's good and bad in everything. So, be as objective as possible and write a list of things you believe yourself to be good at and a list of things you would describe as your weak points. Now, look at the list of weaknesses: Is there anything on there that you would like to be good at? Thanks to the human's ability to fluidly change our abilities, you can be! You don't have to be perfect, but you can get a jolt of positivity by attempting something you may have written off as a weakness and improving that skill even slightly.

- **Surround yourself with good people.** If you are someone who is developing a new version of yourself and wants to find new passions in life, you will need the right people surrounding you for support. If someone drains you of your positivity— through constant negative reassurance—they are probably holding you back. Try to surround yourself with people who uplift and inspire you, as well as those who make the effort to create positive change within their own lives.

- **Don't feel guilty about your happiness.**
  Start prioritizing your joy. You can do this by putting time aside every day to do something you love just for you. Once you start prioritizing your happiness you will see the critical need for boundaries. So, go out there and try out that restaurant you've been eyeing for the past year, go on a trip with your best friend, or start learning a new language!

As you start improving other areas of your life, you will begin to realize the importance of having firm boundaries. You might even start noticing just how much you used to do for others while putting your own happiness on the back burner.

Key Takeaways

- Ego is about the blind belief that one is better than another, while self-esteem is about knowing one's true worth.
- The self-worth theory describes four key components that dictate how we value ourselves: ability, effort, performance, and self-worth.
- If you are insecure about yourself, working toward a place of neutrality is the first step in gaining more confidence.

- Developing good self-esteem has to do with believing in your ability to conquer adversity—don't shy away from a challenge.
- Accepting compliments is important for your sense of self-worth and becoming comfortable with others acknowledging it.
- Improving surrounding areas of your life will directly boost your self-esteem as your overall satisfaction increases.

Chapter 6
Setting Boundaries Starts with You

Healing may not be so much about getting better, as about letting go of everything that isn't you—all of the expectations, all of the beliefs—and becoming who you are.

— Rachel Naomi Remen

As you might have grasped by now, setting boundaries has more to do with ourselves than others. By understanding ourselves and facing our own demons, we become better at setting healthy boundaries.

Reasonable boundaries come from a place of respect, value, and love. Manifestations of deep insecurities, on the other hand, are nagging feelings that make you feel unworthy without anyone else's wrongdoing. These little pesky insecurities get the best of us, which is why every once in a while, we'll feel like we're getting eaten up with an emotion we don't want to feel in the first place. To create healthier boundaries, we first need to figure out whether our needs are representative of something *we* need to work on or if it's something that concerns others.

Shadow Work and You

Shadow work, a practice developed by the famed Swiss psychologist Carl Jung, is a method that helps one answer questions they are often afraid of asking themself, thus freeing them from their secrets and allowing them to identify the boundaries they would want to set. The great thing about shadow work is that it is highly customizable and you can practice it for years without reaching the end of its usefulness. Getting to know yourself is a never-ending process.

According to Jung, each one of us has a persona. Think of this as the mask we wear to project a certain image of ourselves to the outside world. We also each have a shadow side. Our shadow tends to be the opposite of this conscious personality and can be instinctive and irrational.

Shadow work is meant to unveil what is beneath that mask, specifically the parts of ourselves that we tend to reject and generally cover-up. For example, having aggressive or mean tendencies would certainly be something that the persona of a hyper-agreeable person would try to mask, as they don't want to be associated with such attributes.

These darker parts of ourselves can be quite frightening to acknowledge and confront—even admitting to ourselves that we have them can be difficult to get through. However, by giving these darker parts of yourself attention through shadow work, you will be taking away their power and getting in touch with what you actually want to express.

To get started with some basic shadow work, sit down in a calm environment with a journal and a pen, and start answering these questions:

- Do I feel like I treat myself with kindness and respect—the same way I should expect someone else to treat me?
- Do I often allow others to treat me with less kindness and respect than I deserve?
- What are some examples of healthy and happy relationships that I've witnessed? What do I like about them?
- What are some examples of unhealthy relationships that I've witnessed? What were the issues?
- How easy is it for me to see someone for exactly who they are without unrealistically idolizing them?
- Do I struggle to confront a person when they have done me wrong? If so, what feelings do I experience at the thought of confronting them?
- What do I feel when my best friend seems to be spending more time with their other friends than with me? What is/would be my reaction?
- How easily do I get jealous in romantic relationships?
- Can I easily and neutrally accept the fact that my romantic partner has been with other people before me?

- Can I easily and neutrally accept the fact that my ex is with other people following our breakup?
- Am I holding on to any feelings or resentment from my past relationships? If so, what are they, and why is it so difficult for me to let go of them?
- Do I truly believe I am being realistic when it comes to wanting a relationship? Do I expect them to be perfect and solve all of my problems or do I understand that relationships are never perfect and require work from both parties?

It is important to understand that your shadow is not a shortcoming or a mistake, but rather an inherent part of who you are. Ultimately, the goal of shadow work is to gain self-awareness. It enables you to recognize the various parts of yourself. When we start to embrace these darker parts of ourselves, we obtain control and can start showing up as our authentic selves.

Setting Boundaries with Yourself

We tend to think of boundaries as a way to communicate our limits with others, but we also need to consider the boundaries we set for ourselves. These boundaries enable us to uphold a certain lifestyle, maintain stability, and stay healthy.

Everyone has their own set of boundaries. The limits you set for yourself might be very different from others, but let's take a look at some examples to give you a general idea of what your boundaries could be:

- Sticking to a budget

- Not answering work emails on the weekends
- No phones or TV allowed in the bedroom
- Not using social media when you're bored
- Avoiding unhealthy foods
- Having no more than 2 cups of coffee a day
- Not drinking alcohol during the week

The majority of us struggle to keep certain self-imposed limits. We all understand the benefits of discipline and limitations, yet it can be challenging to follow them. However, when we change our perception and start to understand these boundaries as a means to achieve our goals, perhaps we can view them in a better light. You're not depriving yourself from having a bag of Doritos, you're working on becoming healthier. You're not missing out on a chance to let loose with friends, you are prioritizing rest. Boundaries around the things that interfere with our goals allow us to ultimately live a happier life.

Your Inner Child

Some of us must use self-imposed boundaries as a means to *re-parent* ourselves. That's to say, we are providing ourselves with the limits that might have been lacking in our childhood.

As children, we are subject to whatever conditions our parents or guardians put us in. We have very little say in the matter as we are too young to be independent. We are completely reliant on those who hold the responsibility to take care of us.

If you were lucky, your parents had healthy boundaries themselves and taught you to internalize the ability to set healthy boundaries as well. But in reality, most childhoods are flawed in some way or another. I like to believe that every parent does the best they can for their children, but this is of course limited by a parent's own abilities and shaped by their life experience. We pass down the things we know - the good, the bad and the ugly.

Many times, we are well aware of our limits and know when we don't agree with something. However, we struggle to say 'no' in these situations and often end up agreeing anyway; we know we should've declined and may even beat ourselves up for not having the courage to do so. Such compliance and fear of conflict is often rooted in deeper-set issues that stem from the way we were treated as children.

Our primary caretaker might've been too busy at work to provide us with the quality time we needed, might've been too stressed to be emotionally present, or might have even been struggling with a mental health issue that rendered them emotionally unpredictable. A plethora of possibilities can stunt our development and instill the need for constant reassurance, fear of abandonment, excessive people-pleasing, trust issues, and an inability to set boundaries.

Let's explore some of the common childhood conditions that produce emotional difficulties into adulthood. These are important factors to evaluate in your own life to recognize the potential root of your struggles:

1. Your guardian was often too busy to spend adequate time with you. If as a child you were always looking to spend even a sliver of time with a parent you loved but didn't get to see enough, you might develop an overly demanding emotional

attachment to others. You could struggle with the idea of going long periods of time without seeing someone you care about. This could actually cause *them* to set a boundary with you if they felt it was a bit overbearing. You may, on the other hand, need boundaries that protect your need to feel cared for.

2. Your guardian only complimented you and showed you affection when you achieved something. It makes sense for those who are in charge of our growing process to want us to succeed. However, many parents take this to the extreme; they treat their love as a sort of reward. Therefore, it was only expressed to their child if they had achieved something. This form of parenting is harmful and reinforces the idea in a child's mind that they must be successful in areas predetermined by their parents in order to deserve to receive love. This doesn't take into account the differences in people's capabilities, interests, and emotional needs. In adulthood this often manifests as over-achievement, doing things solely for the approval of others, and valuing the opinions of others more than your own.

3. Your guardians were not happy with you unless you were following the trajectory they created for you. I've seen many overbearing parents like this; they live vicariously through their children and cannot accept them as individuals that are separate from them. They expect their children to do just as well in school, love the same things, and do well in the areas they have (or haven't!) excelled at. When they grow up, these kids might not only have a lost sense of identity, but they may succumb

to extreme people-pleasing because it's the only
way to make sure they receive the love they seek.

4. Your guardians often compared you to others or
belittled your individuality. Demanding autonomy
is difficult. Saying no is also very difficult. If these
skills aren't given the space to blossom in one's
early stages of life, they become particularly hard
to develop. If a child was often made to feel
inferior or as if they could never be as good as
others, they struggle to develop the confidence and
self-esteem to believe that their 'no' holds value.

Parents and teachers are our first examples of what it means
to be an adult. In a perfect world, they demonstrate good
conflict resolution, clear communication, mutual respect,
and care for their peers. But without active parenting, many
lessons can simply glide over a child's head. Adults who
grew up in such childhood conditions might be unable to
rely on or trust others and therefore set either overly aggressive boundaries or become completely reliant on others.

Healing Childhood Wounds

Difficulties from a person's childhood will remain present
for a lifetime. The things ingrained in us during our forma-
tive years will always be with us, and the qualities that
prevent us from engaging with the world in healthy ways
must be addressed. We are presented with two options: to
suppress our childhood pain and allow it to continue to
poison our lives, or take some difficult steps to confront that
pain, make peace with it and put it in its place so we can
grow beyond our past.

The fear of abandonment, fear of rejection, difficulty trusting others, co-dependence, and similar issues interfere with our ability to form strong bonds and nurture healthy relationships. By addressing these things, you make it easier for yourself to live the life you desire.

Therapist Andrea Brandt (2018) outlines a step-by-step method of starting to process your childhood wounds:

1. **Connect with yourself.** Begin this process by grounding yourself, your body, and your mind. Simply sit quietly in a comfortable position and bring attention to all of your bodily sensations. Close your eyes, take some deep breaths, and allow your body and mind to be present in that moment. Center yourself by feeling a flow of energy move from the bottom of your spine, into the ground, and all the way into the layers of the earth.

2. **Recall an emotional reaction.** Now that you are present with yourself, think back to a recent incident that produced undesirable feelings within you. It could be when you felt disrespected by a coworker, jealous of your partner, resentful toward a friend, or disappointed by a family member—anything that made you feel unpleasant. Review what led up to you being upset and what about it made you feel the way you did. Notice the details and visualize yourself living through that moment all over again. When you successfully do this to the point of bringing those emotions back up to the surface, proceed to the following step.

3. **Sense the emotions.** As the emotions start to become stronger, allow yourself to sense them

throughout your entire body. Try to pinpoint any physical responses to these emotions that you might be experiencing—tingling, tension, pain, etc. As you scan your body and find these physical sensations, try to carefully describe them to yourself. As soon as you feel that you've identified and described all appropriate physical sensations, you can carry on.

4. **Attach a name to it.** Now, try to identify what each emotion is. If you felt your arms tense up, is this because of anger or frustration? Is the tingling sensation in your chest jealousy? Is your breath feeling shallow because you feel anxious or as if you are in danger? Try to name the emotions that you feel associated with your body's reactions. Go as far as you can to get to the core emotion. For example, "I am disappointed in my friend because she forgot to call me on my birthday" could mean "I am sad because it appears she doesn't care about me".

5. **Assess the situation.** Is this emotion valid? Following the previous example, you could ask yourself: Was it my friend's intention to hurt me? Does she really not care about me? Or are there other possible reasons why she might have forgotten my birthday? Quite possibly you can think of a million possibilities why she forgot to call you. But why do you think you went straight for the worst possible reason? It is worth noticing here that we often don't respond to a situation, we respond to our interpretation of what's happening. Most likely, this situation triggered something in

you that is rooted in something that happened to
you in the past.

6. **Comfort yourself.** It's difficult to love someone
that causes us pain, but what if that someone is
yourself? We might, at a deep level, believe we're
not worthy of love and respect. Recognize that
whatever you have gone through in the past needs
acknowledgment and validation. You needed and
deserved love at that moment. The beautiful thing
is that you can give it to yourself at this very
moment. Love yourself even with all the difficult
emotions that you experience.

7. **Embrace all of it.** These feelings are there for a
reason and they aren't going to go away instantly. So,
sit with them and allow yourself to feel them in full.
Don't lie to yourself about not feeling them, don't
judge them, and don't minimize how strongly you
feel them—just feel them from a point of neutrality.
This might take a while, but only move on to the
next step when you feel like you've truly felt all of
your emotions in full and given them validation.

8. **Learn the lessons.** The emotions you
experience are part of a bigger picture; They are
telling you something you need to change about
either your environment and your life or about
yourself. For this step, dig deep within those
emotions and try identifying other circumstances
that triggered you to feel this way. Notice any
patterns, and if you do see similarities, try to get to
the very root of the problem and figure out why
these situations have such an impact on you.

Dealing with our childhood wounds can be an intimidating and vulnerable task, but we have to remind ourselves that it all lies in the past. We are adults now and are no longer limited by our young age or the need to follow others' authority. We can heal the parts of ourselves that were damaged when we were younger and can learn to stand up for ourselves as adults.

Key Takeaways

- Setting boundaries healthy requires self-reflection.
- Shadow work uses powerful questions to allow you to learn your own needs and assess your satisfaction in your relationships.
- We need to change our perspective on the boundaries we set with ourselves - they are there to help us achieve what we authentically want.
- The way we were treated by adults when we were children can influence how we treat others in adulthood.
- Wounds that are left throughout our childhood manifest in conflict and insecurities when we become adults—it is necessary to acknowledge them and heal them.

Chapter 7
How to Go About It

Daring to set boundaries is about having the courage to love ourselves even when we risk disappointing others.

— Brené Brown

We've figured out the what and the why, but now it is time to get into the *how*. Practically, we have yet to test our theory. Getting around to setting the boundaries can take a while as it can be nerve-wracking, as this is the point where we break out from the comfort zone.

Regaining Your Individuality

First, let's get one thing straight: your life is yours to live. Sometimes, even the hardest of decisions may be necessary for you to preserve your well-being. Once you start valuing your individuality, you will start realizing your worth.

In the previous chapters, we talked about the difference between rational boundaries and emotionally-clouded boundaries. Ideally, your boundaries should genuinely represent your value system and apply those values to the relationships in which you participate. When your boundaries come from a healthy place, then you need not worry about situations that expose your misalignment with others. For example, if you are the type to diligently structure your schedule, you shouldn't feel bad about saying 'no' to a last-minute invitation or request for your help.

Maintaining your individuality in relationships is crucial for your health. In order to do so we must uphold three things: independence, autonomy, and our own point of view (Firestone, 2018). We should have a good sense of who we are inside and outside of all our relationships—you shouldn't be defined by another person's expectations of you.

Here are a few pointers on how to strengthen your sense of self to prevent it from being mangled by others:

- Try to make more personal decisions without heavily relying on the input of others. If you're wondering whether you should quit your job and find a new career path, for example, make the decision based on your own perception. Yes, of course you could ask others for their input, but don't overly rely on their opinions. After all, everyone will present you with a different perspective. Trust yourself because you are the only person with all the facts of the matter, and you alone are capable of knowing what you truly want.

- You do the things you choose not to satisfy others, but because they fulfill you. It can be difficult to completely detach yourself from other people's feelings, but you can always start small. Pick up a hobby that you've always wanted to try even if you think your peers will find it lame. Satisfy your own needs without being responsible for their feelings about it. If *you* enjoy something, you deserve to spend your time doing it.

- You are at peace with your own feelings. If you are upset, you can generally uncover the root cause; if you feel uncomfortable in a certain situation, you don't push those feelings down. Being well-versed in your own emotional world is needed to prevent others from swaying you. Don't let others gaslight you into thinking you aren't feeling what you're feeling.

- You are aware of your various identities, and they all make you feel positive. You can be a mother, a teacher, a CEO, a musician, a farmer, etc. There is no cap on how many identities you can assign yourself. What's more important than their quantity is their relevance to who you really are.

- You feel in control of your life. Now, this is a tricky one because, at times, life is out of our control. Major life events come up that must be dealt with, and we can find ourselves barreling toward a situation we never wanted or envisioned. Even when that happens, it is up to us to get back on track.

Taking Back Control

Big life events could derail us temporarily, but having a clear vision with defined goals helps us stay the course. I've worked with many clients whose dreams have been derailed due to sudden life events like caring for a terminally-ill loved one. Beyond time constraints, these situations take up so much mental and emotional bandwidth it can feel impossible to take on any other commitment.

There is a story from my childhood about crossing a rushing river that has stuck with me over the years, and I believe it is an apt metaphor for when life becomes chaotic. I was ten years old and my eldest brother had taken me with him to a little island in the middle of a river near our home. We crossed the river for about 50 yards to reach a sandy beach by hopping from rock to rock. My brother's friends joined later and I decided I was ready to go home. He sent me on my way, pointing out the shallowest path across. The water moved fast and many of the rocks were slippery, but he assured me I would be okay and that he would be watching. Nonetheless, I was scared.

I carefully made my way through the water and over rocks, but about halfway back to the riverbank I lost my footing and fell into the cold water. The current washed me onto a nearby rock. I clambered out of the water and sat down, completely seized up in fear. Looking back at the island and forward to the bank, I suddenly felt alone, overwhelmed, and incapable. Here I was, in the middle of a strong current, washed away from the path to safety with no clear way back. Frankly, I was furious with my brother for putting me in this situation in the first place.

Abandoning my pride, I began to scream for help. Angry and afraid, my cries caught my brother's attention and he bolted off in my direction. I watched him leap effortlessly from rock to rock, eventually swimming up to the one I had perched myself on. He jumped out of the water and put his hand on my head, giving me a little squeeze and telling me I could calm down. We paused for a moment to allow my hysterics to subside. In typical fashion of the eldest child of a family, my brother wanted to impart a lesson as we moved through the water:

"The river is the same as life. The water level will change, and the strength of the current will fluctuate, but the water will never stop flowing. You can cry on this rock all day and you'll still be stuck in the middle of the river."

Of course, this only fueled my rage at him, but at least I was no longer alone in the situation. Someone more experienced had arrived to help me out. My brother explained the plan to help calm me down:

"You got washed off the easy path, so we need to figure out how to get across. We can't swim against the current, so let's look downstream and let the river take us to the next rock."

My heart raced as we jumped into the river. The water was icy cold and I was terrified the current would suck me away. We arrived at the next rock as promised, and sat there to warm up before taking the next plunge. The rock made me feel safe and grounded. I knew the water continued to rush past me but, in that moment, I could breathe easier.

The next time we had to swim, I felt safer and more confident. When we eventually made it to the riverbank, we hiked back up to the path I would follow to our house.

You see, when life becomes chaotic, we can't stop living it; we must find ways to exist within the chaos by carving out a space, however minuscule, to regain our footing. We may need to ask for help and take a circuitous route to arrive at the final destination, but as long as we are making steps in the right direction we've got to trust the process.

Keisha was a client of mine two years into a three-year Master's degree program. Her husband had been in a terrible accident and was rendered unable to work or care for himself, requiring Keisha to not only manage his recovery but also return to an old job to make up for the lost income. She had abandoned her dreams, money was tight and she was emotionally drained.

Among the many challenges this situation presented, Keisha's main concern with me was overcoming a crippling feeling of powerlessness and a growing pattern of negative thinking. She had risen to the occasion and wouldn't have had it any other way, but at a point she did not know where to turn for help; she was paralyzed. She found herself completely sidelining her own life out of a sense of obligation to the person she loved most.

What Keisha needed in order to change her mindset was to first validate her unpleasant feelings. Her negative thoughts did not stem from bitterness or selfishness, but from authentic disappointment and a bleak outlook on the future she had envisioned. It was okay to feel desperate and even angry. We needed to break the situation into manageable chunks to create a fresh perspective of these new circumstances. Instead of looking at the bigger picture, we looked at small ways to restore a sense of agency in her life. This resulted in her enlisting family members to help with the care of her husband, coming to an arrangement with her Master's program to complete her coursework online, and even taking time for herself to see friends again. She found small ways to feel comfort in the midst of all the pain.

We are largely in control of our own future, but we are subject to time and chance as well. Giving yourself time to mourn, grieve, and regroup is necessary, but there comes a moment when we must reestablish, and possibly modify, our original goals and vision. Even in an all-consuming situation, we must find a rock that can shield us from the chaos.

Training Assertiveness

Before we get to the part where you unleash your assertiveness, let's pinpoint one thing: there's a distinct line between assertiveness and aggression. Assertiveness has everything to do with communicating your wants and needs while respecting the wants and needs of others. Aggressiveness, on the other hand, comes from a desire to control. To be assertive is to confidently express yourself while listening to others. Aggressiveness is disrespectful and features one person placing the importance of their desires over the wants and needs of someone else. Many of us confuse asserting ourselves with being aggressive, so it is important to differentiate the two.

On the other end of that spectrum, we have passiveness, a chronic characteristic in people who tend to avoid conflict. Again, this stems from them not being confident in their individuality—as if their needs and wants are always less important than others'.

You might convey passive behavior if you say things such as "no, it's okay—you decide this time," except it isn't just that one time and you might actually say this more often. In your mind, you don't feel strongly about the choice presented to you. Or you're simply too afraid of getting a negative response. Doing this too often may cause people to start thinking that it's okay to make your decisions for you. Furthermore, it sends out the message that your needs can be freely bulldozed by someone else. Being too passive hurts you in the long run.

It may seem difficult for someone who has become accustomed to passive behavior to suddenly flip a switch. Many people have a naturally passive personality and that quality serves them well! Being decisive and able to assert yourself with confidence, however, is an essential skill set in life and in setting boundaries. Here are a few things you can do to get going:

- Voice a dissenting opinion about a non-controversial topic.
- Be simple and direct.
- Leave negative emotions out of it.
- Use 'I' statements to solidify the fact that you deserve to be respected.
- Don't be surprised if others react negatively to your newfound assertiveness and give them space to be upset without taking ownership of their feelings.
- Be mindful of your body language: stand tall, push your shoulders back, and try to maintain eye contact rather than look down or away.

Here are two examples of situations in which you could assert yourself more:

- **Practice being less lenient with your work life**. It seems as though the word 'boss' makes people feel as if they have power over how one spends their time. Although society reinforces this notion, no one's boss should push them around. If your boss or even other coworkers have gotten used to you picking up their slack or always being available, they will continue adding work to your pile. To fix this, let them know of your intentions in a way that respects the person but indicates that you will be making your own decisions from now on. For example, when your boss asks you to stay late for an extra thirty minutes, try providing a solution that caters better to your needs. For example, you could say something along the lines of "Unfortunately I can't stay in longer today. I have some personal things I must tend to, but I'll be glad to pick this up tomorrow." With a response like that, you're saying 'no' in a way that doesn't burn any bridges. You're not asking permission to do this task tomorrow, you are posing a reasonable solution that respects both your time and the work that needs to be done.

- **Stand up to your loved ones in disagreements.** Yes, sometimes it's easier to let conversations flow naturally and not even get involved with your own opinions. However, to get comfortable with being assertive, you have to practice speaking up in *all* situations. If your family members are having a discussion about something and are presenting opinions different from yours, force yourself to chime in. No, I'm not encouraging you to instigate fights or heated arguments. Simply allow others to get accustomed to respecting your opinion. You could say, "I see what you are saying, but I actually see it differently". The key here is to keep the focus on your opinion rather than disagreeing with their point of view. Speak from your perspective by using "I" and "me". As long as you stay respectful and do not denigrate the opinions of others, you can always establish your assertiveness.

There's no reason to be ashamed of a lack of assertiveness, considering that it isn't completely natural to the majority of people. As a child, you almost always have to say 'yes'—to your parents, your teachers, or any other people superior to you. Many of us carry this passiveness well into adulthood.

The Art of Saying No without Guilt

Saying 'no' is hard. It can make you feel guilty, embarrassed, and leave you feeling like you're letting someone down. But, in reality, saying no rarely leads to battles or blood feuds. And it's more common and less risky than you think.

The art of saying no has everything to do with getting comfortable with 'no' and experiencing that saying no isn't as bad as you might have envisioned it. The more comfortable we get with it, the easier it will become, trust me.

We often feel guilty when we say 'no', because we feel responsible for the other person's reaction. We would rather avoid any conflict that might occur, safeguarding ourselves from a big fight, being made to feel selfish, or even worse, someone leaving us. In reality, however, saying 'no' to others and 'yes' to ourselves is perceived as a strength. When people are comfortable saying 'no' when needed, it elicits tremendous respect from those around them. They tend to be described as more reliable and dependable than their over-extended counterparts. Their 'yes' carries more weight as a result.

Guilt arises when we have done something wrong. Unearned guilt, however, is a concept those of us with difficulty setting boundaries are susceptible to. This is when one feels guilty about something they are not responsible for.

There are several reasons we succumb to unearned guilt, both internal and external. Some of us feel naturally responsible for the well-being of certain people in our lives, effectively blurring the line between empathy and guilt. An example of this would be allowing a friend going through a difficult time to lean on you to the point you need to cut other commitments out of your schedule. Others may experience being guilt-tripped as a result of unhealthy relationship dynamics. No matter the root source of unearned guilt, it is crucial to examine the validity of that feeling. True guilt only applies when we have violated another person's well-being due to a situation we have created. To release ourselves from the burden of guilt we must change the story we tell ourselves.

Based on what you've read so far, do you believe that forming boundaries makes you selfish? Does creating a boundary constitute some action that will result in a harmful outcome? Or is it perhaps a lack of boundaries that has you taking responsibility for a problem you did not create?

To help you on your way with saying 'no', there are a couple of things you can start doing:

- **Start noticing how often we say 'no'.** On rare occasions, someone gets angry when someone else says 'no'. If you make it a habit to start noticing how normal it is to say 'no' in conversations, you will see that it seldom leads to anger and rage. By consciously bringing your attention to these indistinct interactions, you are telling your mind that saying 'no' doesn't have to be problematic.
- **Make a counterproposal.** We don't always have to say 'no'. Sometimes it's just a matter of changing the request. When someone asks us to do something we might think we only have two options, responding with *yes* or *no*. By making a counteroffer to a request we take back control and insert our own needs. That could look something like this: "I would love to help you move this weekend, but I can only help you for two hours."
- **Buy yourself time.** If someone asks us to do something, we are not required to answer immediately. Buying time is a great way to alleviate yourself from making hasty decisions. Simply saying "I'll think about it," or "Let me get back to you on that," will immediately increase your sense of control. 'Maybe' is also an acceptable

answer when you are unsure if you genuinely have the time to commit to their request.

- **Having a rule about something.** I personally use this one very often, especially when it comes to touchy topics. When someone asks you to borrow money it can be hard to answer with a blunt 'no'. Saying something like "I'm sorry I have a rule about not lending money" or "I'm sorry I can't come, we always have family dinner on Thursday nights" adds weight to your 'no'. Being told something is non-negotiable has a powerful effect. Try it out and see how disarming this simple statement can be.

Saying 'no' takes practice and it might feel uncomfortable in the beginning, but you'll see how fast it'll become your second nature once you get used to it. Get used to saying "this is non-negotiable" if you find yourself being pushed around.

Having Tough Conversations

Even if you might be the shyest person you know, the best way to handle difficult conversations is to just rip the band-aid off. In this case, it means you need to face the conversation head-on. Trust me, tiptoeing about what you truly want to say will only increase your nervousness in the moment.

Try bringing up a minor issue that bothered you by being objective and clear. Make sure you understand *why* you are bringing this issue up. Yes, your feelings may have been hurt or perhaps you felt disrespected, but what is the goal you're trying to achieve? Do you seek validation? Or are you looking for a change in the other person's behavior?

When I started out setting healthy boundaries and needed to have hard conversations, I would always prepare before I talked to the other person. It helped me calm down, gather my thoughts, center myself, and even solidify my sense of self-worth. I defined my goal for the conversation and examined my emotions, validating my reason for bringing the matter up in the first place. Once prepared, I would take a walk, go to a park, or have a cup of coffee; anything that would help me speak from a place of calm. By preparing and expelling any strong emotions before the conversation, I found myself speaking more confidently.

Let's go over how a conversation about boundaries should unfold:

1. You find a time that is comfortable for both you and the other person. Make sure the time you've scheduled to talk is adequately long and isn't immediately following a stressful day at work, for example. You want both parties to be in emotionally stable moods to perceive the conversation objectively.
2. You start by saying you have come to the conclusion that this conversation is necessary for the two of you to continue the relationship in a healthy manner. You should add that you haven't been satisfied with how things are going, and the objective of this conversation is to resolve these issues—not to attack the other person out of spite.
3. Be very clear about the boundaries you have chosen to set. In other words, don't leave them up

to interpretation. Instead of using phrases sounding like "I think what could be good is...", which make your opinions sound more like passive suggestions, say "what I need to change in order to feel good in this relationship is...".

4. Explain the reasoning behind your boundaries. In this case, the explanation is not offered as justification, but as a means for the other person to recognize why this change is required of them. Make sure not to downplay the effect of the other person's previous actions; say "when you do things like that, I feel unheard, hurt, and disrespected. I don't want to feel those things around someone I care so much about, which is why I'm introducing these boundaries and asking for a change."

5. Answer questions, as long as they are being asked respectfully. If the other person needs some further clarification on a certain boundary, provide it to them. After all, you both want to leave this conversation on the same exact page. After you've explained what your boundaries are and why you are setting them, you can discuss the details such as when they apply and how you would like them to handle these changes.

6. Listen to the other person without excusing them. When you've laid out your side, the person you're talking to might want to provide their perspective. You can listen to what they have to say and notice if they are taking accountability. If all you hear are excuses and justifications, they are likely avoiding this chance to confront their own flaws. In such a case, you will want to steer the conversation back

to how their actions made you feel in the past. Make it clear you are not seeking an apology or an explanation. You simply want to maintain this relationship but need to see some changes if it is to continue.

7. If they have been responding positively and have acknowledged the past in the way you've described it, consider opening up the conversation to their boundaries as well. If it feels right, ask the person if there are any insufficient aspects of the relationship from *their* point of view and listen to them with the same understanding they offered you.

8. Make sure you both have fully understood the new requirements for the relationship and feel free to end the conversation.

The bottom line of the conversation is asserting your needs. The goal is for you to lead the conversation from a place of compassion and remain in the driver's seat. It will surely be difficult to initiate a conversation like this, and it could easily be derailed if the other person is focused on explaining or excusing their behavior - or worse, invalidating what you are attempting to tell them. Ideally, you both leave the conversation with a deeper understanding of each other as individuals and resolute to improve upon the relationship. This won't always be the case, so what can you do when your assertiveness is met with disrespect? You have, after all, found the courage to be vulnerable by expressing your feelings. It is important to realize that by allowing yourself to be vulnerable, you are also tapping into the vulnerabilities of the other person. This type of conversation could be met with defensiveness, hurt, or aggression if the other person is not ready to address some of the difficult feelings this brings up.

It is important to understand that their reaction isn't your responsibility. You initiated a conversation from a place of compassion with the intention of bettering the relationship. Any negative reaction to that could be a form of resistance, stem from their own personal issues, or simply because they're having a bad day. My point here is that there are plenty of possible reasons why they might be angry, hurt, or defensive, and those possible reasons are valid, but their reaction is not something for you to solve. If the conversation gets too heated, you can always firmly set another boundary "This is non-negotiable. I will not be yelled at, let's continue this conversation when you are ready to talk."

Key Takeaways

- To stop over-compromising it is important to make doing things for yourself a priority.
- Major life events can drag us completely off course, but there is always help and an alternative route to get you back on track.
- Setting boundaries requires confidence as well as assertiveness
- Developing assertiveness requires small changes in the way you respond to people.
- Assertiveness is exercised when you stop being lenient with others' demands, stand up for your own opinions, and learn to say 'no.'
- Having difficult conversations requires understanding and patience from both parties.

- Accept the outcome of your conversation regardless of the other person's reaction; the only goal for now is that you clearly assert yourself.

Chapter 8
Sticking to Your Boundaries

Do not justify, apologize for, or rationalize the healthy boundary you are setting. Do not argue. Just set the boundary calmly, firmly, clearly, and respectfully.

— Crystal Andrus

You've found the courage to initiate a difficult conversation with someone you care about. You took an important step toward preserving the relationship by voicing your needs. Pat yourself on the back because this is something some of us will never find the strength to do! Reactions will vary and you may find yourself navigating a period of instability as this sinks in with those around you. It is possible that one conversation is all it takes with some people, yet others may challenge your assertiveness or find difficulty upholding your requests.

Old habits die hard! Your work is probably not over after that first conversation and you may have to continuously reinforce the boundary you have set. Be patient with those around you but firm in your resolve. Time and experience will impart greater confidence if you stick to your guns.

Noticing the Changes

Most people are neither completely good nor totally bad. Helpful and destructive, vulnerable yet powerful, capable of both inflicting and feeling pain, we are complex beings unable to be labeled by a simplistic binary of good or evil. We can acknowledge that good people sometimes do bad things, and vice versa.

Our personalities are not static, and certain characteristics will be enhanced or suppressed depending on our environment. A particular work culture may develop leadership skills while suppressing creativity. A certain person may bring out your sense of humor but you have trouble being serious around them. The interplay between our personality and the traits of those around us creates the dynamic that defines how that relationship plays out.

It's safe to say that some personalities simply clash. Constant arguing or a general apathy toward one another makes it clear some people are just not a match and will probably never form a strong bond with each other. But what about a family relationship that has soured? Or a romantic relationship that started off great but has recently begun taking more from you than it gives? Perhaps a manager or colleague has become difficult to work with, yet you must find a way to carry on. It's easy to avoid becoming close with people who are clearly not a match, but when you begin asserting yourself and establishing boundaries in the later stages of a relationship, conflict may arise.

When you begin setting boundaries, telling people 'no', and asserting your opinions, you'll receive a wide array of reactions from those around you. Relationship dynamics are bound to change as your newfound confidence manifests.

Some people will become super fans and compliment you on the fact that you've found your voice. Others may react with ambivalence. And then there are those who will begin to pull away, behave (passive) aggressively toward you, or otherwise create a palpable tension in the air. Pay close attention to the changes occurring around you - who treats you differently and how?

To Be With or Not to Be With

We all know that relationships aren't always completely gratifying. Some of us might even consider leading a more solitary life because of it. After all, why expend all that emotional effort attempting to bond with a person whose presence in your life isn't necessary in the first place? Maybe it's easier to not have any friends, cut all ties with your family, and quit looking for a romantic partner.

I can't say it isn't tempting at times to simply shut everyone out. When you're feeling overwhelmed and it feels as though some of your close relationships are going through a tumultuous period, the idea of being left alone might seem heavenly. We are, however, social creatures largely incapable of a solitary existence. We need to work through our issues because the benefits of human connection far outweigh the alternative.

No one's going to be a perfect person—there will be times when they might be unintentionally cold, fail to be there for you, and even lack the willingness to have a heartfelt conversation. It would be unrealistic to expect perfection, but if any relationship causes you more stress than fulfillment, it might be time to reevaluate.

Maintaining Boundaries

Let's discuss what it takes to achieve a lasting change. You've accomplished the first step: vocally asserting your needs. What's required to maintain this new dynamic is enforcing the consequences when your boundaries continue to be overstepped.

Here are four tactics you can apply:

Restating the boundary

When someone goes back on what you agreed upon, you may need to reassert where you draw the line. You were right to speak up and you maintain the right to hold someone to their word. If you notice yourself excusing violations of your boundaries as no big deal, you are slipping back into old habits. Part of the process of maintaining your boundaries is giving them the same priority they had during the initial conversation. You won't sound like a broken record by reminding anyone to respect a boundary. You have placed the onus on them to change their behavior, so repeating your assertion out loud reinforces the issue's importance and proves your resolve. Your mindset will benefit from the double-edged effect of this as well. By asking for a small commitment from someone repeatedly, you will feel increasingly justified in your request.

Enforcing the Consequences

Eventually, enough is enough. If someone continuously oversteps a boundary even after repeated reminders, it is time to create space between you and them. It should be clear by now that this boundary is rock-solid and you will not waver. Let them know that this is the last time you will discuss this boundary with them and inform them of the consequences if they cross the line again. For example, you could say something like "If you break plans with me by not showing up or informing me, I won't go out with you anymore."

Dealing With the Bad

You have begun setting boundaries, standing up for yourself, and taking back control of your life. It may become clear at this point that some relationships will not be able to develop in the way you would have envisioned. That's okay because you have done the hard work of assessing that relationship, shown vulnerability by communicating your deepest feelings, and given someone the opportunity to work with you toward a healthier coexistence.

Let's say you have fully assessed an individual with whom you have a fraught relationship and have concluded their influence over your life must end. They continue to disregard your autonomy, it's clear you won't be able to work together to improve, and they over-exert their influence to negative effects. Clearly, they're not respecting your boundaries which is detrimental for your growth and potentially even your health. You might feel betrayed, neglected, and you just can't be yourself around this person.

Here we'll explore some tactics for dealing with a relationship that is not progressing, despite all your best efforts:

- **Take a break.** Sometimes we need a little space to evaluate whether or not a relationship is worth maintaining. Removing a person from your life for a brief period of time gives you the space to reflect on the relationship and that individual from an objective lens. Although *taking a break* is typically associated with romantic partners, you would be equally justified telling a friend or relative you need some space. It doesn't need to be a drawn-out conversation; you could simply make yourself less available. If you feel any explanation is needed, I would suggest keeping it simple - you need to focus on other things for the time being.

- **Let the relationship fade.** There could be a fine line between disengaging emotionally and becoming passive-aggressive, depending on how this is accomplished. I am not advocating the latter. Instead, remove yourself emotionally or restrict the amount of time you commit, and observe how you feel once this distance has been created. Does the extra space alleviate any stress you previously felt? What, if anything, has changed in the way you treat each other? Is there increased tension or a newfound sense of peace? The end goal is to invest your time in mutually beneficial relationships that empower you. By focusing on the healthy relationships in your life you will naturally have less time for those who do not contribute to your happiness.

- **Make a clean break.** Sometimes we hold on to people because we feel trapped by the fear of losing them. Even when we're not happy in this particular moment, we dread the loneliness we will feel without this person in our life. Yes, there will be a grieving process and you will have to pick up the pieces. You may even find yourself temporarily paralyzed by loneliness after making this decision. We crave familiarity and oftentimes it is easier to put ourselves on autopilot to endure an unhealthy situation simply because it's what we know. Realize that you are deserving of healthy love. Remind yourself that you're not alone, you still have other people around you, and that you're actively moving forward toward a better, brighter future in which you can finally be yourself. You are making space for the healthy relationships in your life to blossom, and those relationships will support you as you move through this difficult moment.

Self-Awareness

As you gain a better understanding of what you need and how to form healthier relationships, you will consequently become more aware of other people's boundaries. Awareness that we, too, can be guilty of overstepping someone else's limits can open the door to improving every relationship in our life.

Are you respecting the boundaries set by others? Acknowledging how difficult it can be to communicate a defined set of boundaries, you might consider whether others in your life could benefit from lobbing a bit of assertiveness in your direction! Admittedly a pointed question: are there any relationships in your life that might be strained by your inability to detect where a boundary exists? Don't overthink it, but you now possess the requisite knowledge to forge healthy relationships built on mutual respect, which gives you a wider perspective.

Self-awareness is developed through your sense of self and accepting the fact you are not and can never be perfect—it's normal and human if someone has a slight issue with you. If you feel that you are self-aware enough to accept your flaws, the next step is addressing them with the help of an outside perspective.

If in question, try asking those around you how happy *they* are with your relationship. Remember to have an open mind and show respect for the opinions they voice. If their experience of the relationship differs from yours, that's okay—it's exactly what this conversation is meant to uncover. Listen to their issues, try to understand their limits, and exert an effort to respect them from this point forward.

Key Takeaways

- Setting boundaries with others is no small feat, so allow yourself to be proud of the steps you've taken to improve your relationships and your life.
- Consistency is key, make sure the person upholds their end of the deal and respects your boundaries continuously.
- Reinforce your boundaries with actions - impose consequences if a boundary is repeatedly violated.

- If someone chooses to not comply with your boundaries, it might be time to end the relationship. Take the time to grieve while acknowledging the fact that it needed to end. Stick to your non-negotiables.
- Apply your knowledge of boundaries to see if there are people in your life who may want to set some boundaries with you as well.

Chapter 9
Enjoying a Fresh Take on Life

You never change your life until you step out of your comfort zone; change begins at the end of your comfort zone.

— *Roy T. Bennett*

It's not easy, but once you take the steps prescribed in this book to set clear boundaries, prepare to reap the rewards! You'll feel a newfound sense of freedom. You'll have time to start up that hobby, side hustle, or passion project that's been sitting on the shelf collecting dust, and the people surrounding you push you forward and support you on this journey. There are certain to be bumps along the way, but your new mindset on how to approach them ease the promise of mental peace at the end of the bumpy road. By seeing our obstacles as opportunities, we turn our problems into progress.

Growth in Discomfort

I'm willing to bet a number of the tactics discussed throughout this book strike you as extremely uncomfortable propositions. It is not easy to depart from the well-trodden path in favor of blazing our own trail toward personal growth. Confronting the inner demons that enable the people around us to overstep our boundaries is not a pleasant task. But growth does not come from a place of comfort. Comfort and growth do not coexist. The way I see it, we're only given two options: spend a lackluster existence living up to the expectations of others, or embrace the challenges and face life head-on.

There's a saying "If you keep doing what you're doing, you'll keep getting what you're getting". Our actions perpetuate themselves, so if we allow someone to violate a boundary once, they are destined to continue doing so. Take the power into your hands by showing you have clear limits about what you'll tolerate, and watch everything else fall into line. Dare to dream big, dare to disagree, and take ownership of your journey. The goal in your path toward personal growth is not to eradicate discomfort, it is to get comfortable with being uncomfortable.

Change often induces fear. Fear of being pulled out of our comfort zone, leaving us fully exposed and vulnerable. However, if we take the metaphor of a hermit crab, we get a better understanding of how discomfort can be a catalyst for growth. Hermit crabs are curious little creatures that shed their exoskeleton several times throughout their lives in a process called *molting*. During this process, the crab's body has grown too big, making it uncomfortable to stay in its shell. They are easy prey and incredibly vulnerable as they seek a new home that fits their larger body. Like the example of the hermit crab, we must allow ourselves to get uncomfortable and put ourselves in danger by 'coming out of our shells', but it is only through this process that we achieve actual growth.

An Oath to Truth

We discussed the two basic human needs of connection and authenticity at the beginning of this book. When those two needs are in balance, we are happy in our lives and in our relationships. We feel the freedom to be ourselves without compromising deep connections with others. People who enjoy the balance of authenticity and connectedness display confidence, good habits, and healthy relationships - all of which fuel the fire to continue improving upon what's already working.

Authenticity is not an endpoint. Rather, it is an ongoing process of being truthful to ourselves in every single moment. It takes constant attention to the root of what makes you, *you* - and focusing on that truth as your north star. Authenticity is not something we need to create or discover. Though we may have buried it deep within, it is merely the truth that exists at the core of our being.

We often praise and value the honesty of children. We attribute it to their innocence and purity and might even say "I wish I could be more like that". Once as a little girl, I looked across the table at Thanksgiving dinner and proclaimed "Aunt Mary got fat!" to the shock and horror of my parents. They immediately and harshly corrected my behavior as everyone turned to observe how Aunt Mary would react. She chuckled with great warmth, looked at me, and said "It's true! I have gotten fatter since I last visited". She wasn't offended because we expect children to speak outrageous truths as they are learning to observe the world around them.

Somewhere down the line, however, we lose that. We are taught it's better to tell a white lie to spare someone's feelings. The more we experience positive feedback as a result of our white lies, the better we get at telling them. Likewise, the more we observe the negative feedback when voicing the truth, the better we get at suppressing it.

Now I'm not romanticizing a childlike innocence or proposing that kind of response to our surroundings as adults. We have the mental capacity to choose our words more carefully and avoid unnecessary conflict and hurt feelings. But instead of lying to someone to keep the peace, we can opt for truthful alternatives.

A dear friend of mine is an actress and recently invited me to her latest play. I find her to be a talented actress and it brings me great joy to support my friend's artistic endeavor while she struts her stuff on stage. Aside from the chance to see her perform, however, the play was perhaps one of the worst I've ever had to sit through. I lit up every time she came out on the stage and she delivered a great performance, in my (honest) opinion. The play itself, however, was a dud (in my humble opinion).

We went out for drinks after the show and I was momentarily at a loss for the right words. When my friend eventually asked, "And, what did you think?" I could have been honest and told her the show failed to keep my attention, the set design was ugly and the lead actor couldn't hold a note.

But it wouldn't have fit the moment and I'm no theater critic anyway. She was clearly thrilled to be part of this show and landing this role was a big accomplishment for her.

My dilemma was how to live up to my oath of truth while not hurting her feelings or belittling her achievement. So I dug deep - I had not gone to the show because I had high expectations of a life-changing theatrical experience; I had gone to see my friend do what she does best, and she nailed it. So I decided on this truth: "I loved seeing you perform, you nailed this role and I am so thrilled you asked me to come."

I didn't feel I was betraying my authenticity by simply focusing on the positive in order to connect with my friend over an achievement she was proud of. Her need for validation is what that moment called for, so we celebrated her success. There came a later conversation where we discussed the merits of the play itself and I was happily honest because she had invited me to share my opinion.

Discovering Yourself

The gift I hope you receive from reading this book is the gift of a greater self-understanding and a sense of integrity toward your true self. When we embrace our authenticity we create a current that allows life to flow in the direction it was always meant to go.

Learning to set boundaries allows your authenticity the space to breathe freely. It is about taking off the mask and becoming confident in your vulnerability. You will become more daring to try new things and might even transform into an entirely different version of *you* - a version you had only dreamt of before. When we hide behind a mask, people can only comment on that mask, so we cannot possibly feel *seen* or fully understood.

By daring to share what truly lights your fire, you allow others the opportunity to profoundly connect with the *real* you. Some will add fuel to the fire and support your growth. Others may try to extinguish it and keep you but a glowing ember full of potential. It is through self-discovery that we can more easily identify the people who fuel our fire and become innately aware of the boundaries needed to protect it.

With integrity to your true self, you become comfortable with being uncomfortable. You stop allowing fear to cloud your judgment of what you know to be right and wrong. You know who you are and what you need.

Listening to Your Intuition

Getting more in tune with your true self will awaken your inner voice. It is that little voice that has been trying to tell you what's right all along. In the process of self-discovery, you will notice your intuition speaking louder and more often as it guides you toward choices, people, and situations that are likely to have a positive impact.

Not to be confused with instinct, which is a one-dimensional pattern of behavior that influences your decision-making, intuition sprouts from the authentic self. Instinct is a natural, hardwired tendency to behave or react in a certain way. Intuition is a deeper understanding. It is the expression of our emotional, spiritual and logical sides all working in perfect harmony.

Intuition is our built-in GPS that is in touch with our true desires and needs and maps out the best path toward them. It tells us: *'just quit that job you hate already!'*, or *'start writing that book you've been fantasizing about'*. But our logical mind takes over in an effort to protect us. We tend to succumb to the fear of failure. We doubt ourselves and become judgemental of our 'crazy' ideas.

Only by actively listening to our intuition do we come closer to a sense of happiness and fulfillment. Ask yourself this: What makes my heart jump? How does it feel once I've embraced that and succeeded? What new doors are opened because of this leap of faith? Do I dare to be bold enough to embrace this dream and make it a reality?

Your brain will present you with fear, shame, and judgment in a valiant yet misguided attempt at self-preservation. Instead, I suggest putting your logical side to work and come up with a set of practical goals that lead you, step by step, toward the dream life you desire.

Key Takeaways

- Healthy and valuable relationships allow you to flourish and grow as a person.
- Improving your life often means getting comfortable with discomfort; step out of your comfort zone to unlock new possibilities.
- Consistent honesty brings us closer to our authentic selves.

- Learning to set boundaries allows your authenticity to thrive.
- Through intuition we already know what we truly desire and need. We just have to be brave enough to listen to it.

Conclusion

Trust yourself, you have survived a lot, and you will survive whatever is coming.

— Robert Tew

I want you to trust yourself. Yes, I can share with you the lessons my own life has taught me, things I've seen other people learn, and the facts that I have come to rely on throughout my professional career, but nothing beats your own intuition, guided by a true understanding of your authentic self. Much of what was written in the past nine chapters is likely something you already know deep down. Sometimes, we might just need someone else to deliver the message in order for it to fully sink in.

The fear that arises when we think about change in our lives often has nothing to do with external factors. Much of the fear we feel about our future has nothing to do with scary possibilities outside of our control. It has everything to do with being afraid of a version of ourselves we don't yet know. We are comfortable when we know who we are; when considering big changes we give up that comfort. We have to agree to abandon this version of ourselves for a new one, which can be terrifying.

A sense of responsibility to be kind and selfless should enrich your life, not make it miserable. If we have grown comfortable allowing people to mistreat us time and again, it will be difficult to confront the reasons why we have tolerated their undue influence over our lives. By firmly asserting our boundaries, we clear up space in our hearts and our minds for the seeds of positivity to sprout. You can be so caught up in pleasing the people who will never truly value your efforts that you might actually miss the people you have been hoping to meet all your life. Do not put yourself in such a position—make that space for yourself.

Realize the power you have to change any situation. It doesn't matter if you don't feel ready, because remember: discomfort is your superpower. The more you accept it and fit it into your life in a healthy way, the easier it will be to handle. Free yourself from the fear of becoming a more powerful *you*. Start living your life through conscious action, even if it means giving up the reality you are used to.

Thank You

Thank you so much for buying my book. I hope it was both informing and insightful.

Before you go, can I ask you for one small favor? **Could you please consider leaving a review on Amazon?**

Your feedback helps independent authors like me to create more books that will hopefully keep on helping you and others.

It would mean the world to me to hear from you.

Get Your Ebook Stop Limiting Yourself
+ Reduce Stress in 1 minute [video]
+ Printable Gratitude Journal

Scan the QR code below to claim your free bonuses

———————————— OR ————————————

visit gifts.zerayoung.com/boundaries

Scan me

Get Ready to Live a Life With No Limits!

✓ Free e-book: Stop Limiting Yourself. Stop doubting your potential and learn to recognize your self-limiting beliefs!

✓ Free meditation video: Reduce your stress levels in one minute with this powerful breathing exercise.

✓ Printable Journal: Print out your daily and monthly Personal Gratitude Journal for positive manifestation and improved self-confidence!

References

20 *inspirational quotes on boundaries*. Jane Taylor | Mindfulness & Compassion Teacher | Mind-Body Connection Coach | Wellbeing Coaching | Mindful Self-Compassion Coaching | Gold Coast. (2021, October 18). https://www.habitsforwellbeing.com/20-inspirational-quotes-on-boundaries/

Ackerman, C. E. (2018, November 6). *What is self-worth & how do we build it? (incl.. worksheets)*. PositivePsychology.com. Retrieved September 22, 2022, from https://positivepsychology.com/self-worth/#what-is

Borreli, L. (2016, March 2). *People-pleaser: Brain scans show pushovers agree with others to avoid mental stress*. Medical Daily. Retrieved September 22, 2022, from https://www.medicaldaily.com/people-pleaser-brain-activity-mental-stress-376139

Brandt, A. (2018, April 2). *9 steps to healing childhood trauma as an adult*. Psychology Today. Retrieved September 22, 2022, from https://www.psychologytoday.com/ca/blog/mindful-anger/201804/9-steps-healing-childhood-trauma-adult

Cherry, K. (2021, September 3). *How to stop being a people-pleaser*. Verywell Mind. Retrieved September 22, 2022, from https://www.verywell-mind.com/how-to-stop-being-a-people-pleaser-5184412

Conley, M. (2022, March 28). *45 quotes that celebrate teamwork, hard work, and collaboration*. HubSpot Blog. Retrieved September 22, 2022, from https://blog.hubspot.com/marketing/teamwork-quotes

Firestone, T. (2018, May 4). *Preserving individuality to strengthen your relationship*. PsychAlive. Retrieved September 22, 2022, from https://www.psychalive.org/preserving-individuality-strengthen-relationship/

Goodreads. (n.d.). *A quote by Dido Stargaze*. Goodreads. Retrieved October 4, 2022, from https://www.goodreads.com/quotes/10881157-if-your-absence-doesn-t-bother-them-then-your-presence-never

Goodreads. (n.d.). *A quote by Shannon L. Alder*. Goodreads. Retrieved October 4, 2022, from https://www.goodreads.com/quotes/70613 8-the-only-real-conflict-you-will-ever-have-in-your

Goodreads. (n.d.). *Boundaries Quotes (451 quotes)*. Goodreads. Retrieved October 4, 2022, from https://www.goodreads.com/quotes/tag/bound-

aries#:~:text=%E2%80%9CWhen%20we%20fail%20to%20set,a%20be-
havior%20or%20a%20choice.%E2%80%9D

Goodreads. (n.d.). *Comfort zone quotes (342 quotes)*. Goodreads. Retrieved
October 4, 2022, from https://www.goodreads.com/quotes/tag/comfort-
zone#:~:text=%E2%80%9CYou%20never%20change%20y-
our%20life,end%20of%20your%20comfort%20-
zone.%E2%80%9D&text=We%20have%20to%20be%20honest,stay%20in
%20our %20comfort%20zone.%E2%80%9D

Goodreads. (n.d.). *Self worth quotes (1650 quotes)*. Goodreads. Retrieved
October 4, 2022, from https://www.goodreads.com/quotes/tag/self-
worth

Klein, Y. (2021, January 20). *How to get over a friendship breakup*. Evolve
Treatment Centers. Retrieved September 22, 2022, from https://evolve-
treatment.com/blog/friendship-breakup/

Lechnyr, D. (2022, June 29). *The consequences of not having any
boundaries*. TherapyDave. Retrieved September 22, 2022, from
https://therapydave.com/self-help/the-consequences-of-not-having-any-
boundaries/

Martin, S. (2020, April 23). *7 types of boundaries you may need*. Psych
Central. Retrieved September 22, 2022, from https://psychcentral.-
com/blog/imperfect/2020/04/7-types-of-boundaries-you-may-need

Morin, A. (2016, June 20). *Compliments make you cringe? science explains
the reasons why*. Inc.com. Retrieved September 22, 2022, from
https://www.inc.com/amy-morin/compliments-make-you-cringe-
science-explains-the-reasons-why.html

Morin, A. (n.d.). *10 signs you're a people-pleaser*. Psychology Today.
Retrieved September 22, 2022, from https://www.psychologytoday.-
com/ca/blog/what-mentally-strong-people-dont-do/201708/10-signs-
youre-people-pleaser

Newhouse, L. (2021, March 1). *Is crying good for you?* Harvard Health.
Retrieved September 22, 2022, from https://www.health.harvard.e-
du/blog/is-crying-good-for-you-2021030122020#:~:text=Re-
searchers%20have%20established%20that%20crying,both%20physical%
20and%20emotional%20pain.

Nitka, D. (2020, August 7). *The importance of setting boundaries*. Connecte
Psychology. Retrieved September 22, 2022, from https://connectepsy-
chology.com/en/2017/05/16/the-importance-of-setting-bound-
aries/#:~:text=In%20the%20context%20of%20psychology,
adult%20is%20responsible%20for%20themselves.

Prism Health North Texas. (n.d.). Establishing healthy boundaries.

Retrieved from http://www.prismhealthntx.org/establishing-healthy-boundaries/

Pangilinan, J. (2022, February 24). *51 quotes about Healing your body & mind* [*2022 update*]. Happier Human. Retrieved October 4, 2022, from https://www.happierhuman.com/quotes-about-healing/

Quotations, S. Q. (n.d.). *The greatest value of having good people around you is not what you get from them but the better person you become because of them... - searchquotes*. Search Quotes. Retrieved October 4, 2022, from https://www.searchquotes.com/quotation/The_greatest_value_of_having_good_people_around_you_is_not_what_you_get_from_them_but_the_better_per/509245/

Santos-Longhurst, A. (2022, March 31). *How to identify your love language*. Healthline. Retrieved September 22, 2022, from https://www.healthline.com/health/love-languages

Subjects. CliffsNotes. (n.d.). Retrieved September 22, 2022, from https://www.cliffsnotes.com/cliffsnotes/subjects/literature/in-which-play-did-william-shakespeare-state-that-misery-loves-company#:~:text=From%2019th%2Dcentury%20American%20essayist,%2C%20misery%20has%20company%20enough.%22

Team, T. S. (2022, September 21). *50 life-changing quotes about trusting yourself*. The STRIVE. Retrieved October 4, 2022, from https://thestrive.co/quotes-about-trusting-yourself/

Waytz, A. (n.d.). *Friend or foe? A psychological perspective on trust*. Friend or Foe? The Psychology of Trust | The Trust Project. Retrieved September 22, 2022, from https://www.kellogg.northwestern.edu/trust-project/videos/waytz-ep-1.aspx

Willis, J., & Todorov, A. (2006, July). *First Impressions: Making up your mind after a 100-MS ... - sage journals*. Retrieved September 23, 2022, from https://journals.sagepub.com/doi/10.1111/j.1467-9280.2006.01750.x

Xplore. (n.d.). *Barbara de Angelis quotes*. BrainyQuote. Retrieved October 4, 2022, from https://www.brainyquote.com/quotes/barbara_de_angelis_119456?src=t_relationship

Xplore. (n.d.). *Marcus Tullius Cicero quotes*. BrainyQuote. Retrieved October 4, 2022, from https://www.brainyquote.com/quotes/marcus_tullius_cicero_156298#:~:text=Marcus%20Tullius%20Cicro%20Quotes&text=Confidence%20is%20that%20feeling%20by%20which%20the%20mind%20embarks%20in,hope%20and%20trust%20in%20itself.